They Call Me Mrs. Job

DONNA DOWIS

ISBN 978-1-64349-968-0 (paperback)
ISBN 978-1-64349-969-7 (digital)

Copyright © 2018 by Donna Dowis

All rights reserved. No part of this publication may be reproduced, distributed, or transmitted in any form or by any means, including photocopying, recording, or other electronic or mechanical methods without the prior written permission of the publisher. For permission requests, solicit the publisher via the address below.

Christian Faith Publishing, Inc.
832 Park Avenue
Meadville, PA 16335
www.christianfaithpublishing.com

The ESV® Bible (The Holy Bible, English Standard Version®) copyright © 2001 by Crossway Bibles, a publishing ministry of Good News Publishers. ESV Text Edition: 2016. The ESV® text has been reproduced in cooperation with and by permission of Good News Publishers. Unauthorized reproduction of this publication is prohibited. All rights reserved.

The ESV® Bible (The Holy Bible, English Standard Version®) is adapted from the Revised Standard Version of the Bible, copyright Division of Christian Education of the National Council of the Churches of Christ in the U.S.A. All rights reserved.

Scripture taken from the NEW AMERICAN STANDARD BIBLE®, Copyright © 1960,1962,1963,1968,1971,1972,1973,1975,1977,1995 by The Lockman Foundation. Used by permission.

The Holy Bible, King James Version. Cambridge Edition: 1769; King James Bible Online, 2018. www.kingjamesbibleonline.org.

Printed in the United States of America

Acknowledgments

Thank you to Christian Faith Publishers, for taking the step of faith and publishing my first book. I will always be grateful to you for seeing a spark of potential.

The writing of any book is a team effort. I have learned much about grammar and perseverance from a great teacher and greater friend. Thank you, Mrs. Joyce Reynolds. Without someone to make webpages, blogs and do PR, books do not get sold. To my goddaughter Amber Walker, thank you from the depths of my heart. I write. My husband types. And a manuscript becomes a book. Steve...because of you I am an author. I thank God for you every day.

Writing this book took years. It was my grief therapy. God's Holy Spirit is my divine Counselor. To Him I am most thankful for His patience and love.

Prologue

Dear Reader:

Mrs. Job has intrigued me for many years. Seemingly, she stands convicted in history as a most undesirable wife. From pulpits around the world, her one statement lifted from context, is ground for condemnation.

Human nature wants to know '*why*' something terrible happens and '*could it be avoided?*' Readers have the advantage over Mr. and Mrs. Job—we know the '*why*' before their story unfolds. To do Mrs. Job (Channa, as I call her) justice, one must step back and consider her circumstances *before* God allowed the devil to attack her home.

She was a wife, married to the greatest man of all the men in the East. Great refers to reputation, as well as wealth and social standing. Job was, by God's declaration, "blameless, upright, feared God and turned away from evil." I suppose you can say Mrs. Job was the Melinda Gates of her time.

Channa was the mother of seven adult sons. By cultural standards, sons left their parental homes to establish their own marital homes. This natural assumption enlarges Channa's family to now include seven daughters-in-law and probably many grandchildren. This lady was also the mother of three daughters, presumably single, because they still lived with their parents and visited the homes of their brothers.

Now consider the intense testing that Channa and Job experience. In one day, they lost all their material wealth and prestige as well as all but three servants. This news is overpowering enough by itself and must be absorbed.

However, that very same day they receive the horrific news that *all* their beloved children who have gathered for a family celebration are now dead. The grief brought wave upon wave of overwhelming assaults upon their already shocked and raw senses. Side by side, with Job's help, she buried every one of her precious and beloved children. How unbelievably broken was the heart of this dear mother.

From her heart and arms, motherhood is violently ripped away.

Wealth and affluence are a memory, instant poverty her new reality.

But wait . . . there is more. Mrs. Job's husband is soon stricken with a most debilitating malady. Then he deserts her—for the city garbage dump, no less. With no cell phone or pony express, how was she to know if he was dead or alive at any given time?

Many, dare I say most, of us would 'crash and burn.'

I do not believe she did.

I propose that her words, "Curse God and die" were not spoken in anger or haste. Rather, she whispered them desperately, sorrowfully, and tearfully from a heart of love and despondency. I think she spoke not only from the bedrock of her faith in God, but out of her confused and raw emotions. If Job angered the Almighty, what was the worst thing God might do? Take Job's life and end his pathetic suffering? There are some things worse than death.

For those of us marked by deep sorrow and grief, we *feel* more than we think. We often speak or react with little forethought. But most of all, we feel as if we stand alone, isolated by unrelenting pain. I am ever grateful that through my deepest and most searing *Valley of the Shadow of Death*, God Almighty held me ever closely to His bosom.

Heavenly Father, when I could not pray, I knew You understood.
When I felt overwhelmed, You gently embraced me.
When I felt I was suffocating, You breathed
upon me Your sweet Spirit.
I praise You for carrying me when I needed You most. Amen.

Romans 8:26—27 (NASB), "In the same way the Spirit also helps our weakness; for we do not know how to pray as we should, but the Spirit Himself intercedes for us with groanings too deep for words. He who searches the hearts knows what the mind of the Spirit is, because He intercedes for the saints according to the will of God."

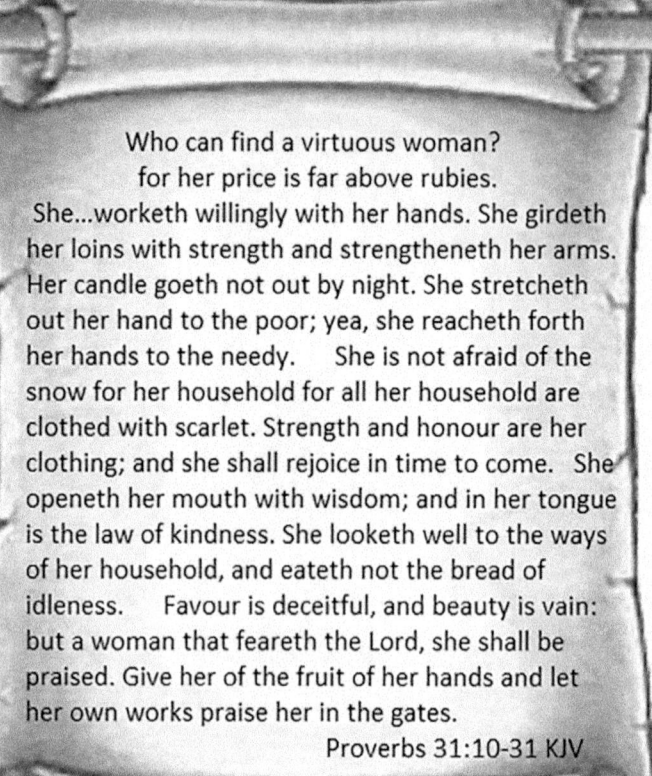

Who can find a virtuous woman?
for her price is far above rubies.
She...worketh willingly with her hands. She girdeth her loins with strength and strengtheneth her arms. Her candle goeth not out by night. She stretcheth out her hand to the poor; yea, she reacheth forth her hands to the needy.   She is not afraid of the snow for her household for all her household are clothed with scarlet. Strength and honour are her clothing; and she shall rejoice in time to come. She openeth her mouth with wisdom; and in her tongue is the law of kindness. She looketh well to the ways of her household, and eateth not the bread of idleness.   Favour is deceitful, and beauty is vain: but a woman that feareth the Lord, she shall be praised. Give her of the fruit of her hands and let her own works praise her in the gates.

Proverbs 31:10-31 KJV

Chapter 1

Who can find a virtuous woman? For her price
is far above rubies. Proverb 31:10

Her eyes scanned the horizon. Dusk was beginning to fall. Shadows teased the landscape. Lifting the beautifully fashioned lamp, Channa trimmed the darkened wick before lighting it. The delicate calming scent of narcissus rose from the pure beaten olive oil. With a smile, she replaced the guiding light in the window. "Shine forth little flame and guide our guests tonight." Turning on her heel, she retrieved a bowl of soup and proceeded to her ailing friend's bedside.

"Open your eyes, dear Adah. I have your broth." Sitting upon the side of the bed, Channa began tenderly spooning the warm nourishment into her nursemaid's chapped lips. The fever had finally broken the day before, and now recovery was possible. Adah looked into the eyes of her beloved mistress and tried bravely to smile. Her exhaustion was evident in her labored breathing. Merely a few years older, Adah had helped birth Channa, and the two of them were inseparable. They could read each other's mind.

Channa knew something was troubling her friend. "Is this broth to your liking?" she asked.

A slight nod affirmed, *yes.* Adah weakly croaked, "The lamp?"

Channa paused, and then nodded her head in understanding. "Our guests are due anytime now. And yes, my precious friend, the lamp is lit and in the window even as we speak." She lifted another spoonful of broth to Adah's lips.

A look of peace spread over Adah's face, now content with the knowledge that the lamp was shining a beacon to strangers. After a few more spoons of broth, Adah began drifting in and out of slumber.

"I must go now. And you must rest," whispered Channa, tucking in the loosely woven blanket around the weakened body of her dearest confidant. Leaning closer, she bestowed a loving kiss upon the brow of her friend. A faint snore was the only response. Quietly, she exited the room pulling the door nearly closed. Even at seventy-five years of age, the darkness still scared Adah.

"Guard her dreams, dear God," she whispered as she slipped down the hallway.

The sound of her guests' imminent arrival quickened her footsteps. Sweeping through her home, she gave a final inspection. All was in order. The noise of snorting camels announced the arrival of her visitors. Raising a hasty hand to her head, she adjusted her hair and slid into her sitting room chair just in time to hear her husband Job greeting their guests outside.

Her daughters, seated nearby, smiled knowingly at her. She winked in agreement. Strangers. Guests for an undetermined length of time. What should they expect? They listened to Job's cordial greetings.

"My friend Eliphaz of Tema, dismount with haste, and welcome back to Shiloh, our home." Job smiled warmly up at his weary guests as they endured the noise and jerks of the kneeling camels. House servants collected the guest's personal belongings. Ranch hands led the now upright camels to nearby corrals for feeding, grooming, and rest. The setting sun cast long shadows across the yard. Ushering their guests inside, Job led them to a spacious reception room where Channa and their daughters were seated patiently waiting.

Motioning to a comfortably plush couch, Job said, "Please rest your tired bodies." Turning to his wife, he began the formal introductions. "My wife, Channa, and our three daughters." The women bowed their heads in acknowledgment and smiled warmly at their guest.

"Welcome to our home," said Channa.

"Thank you, Mrs. Job." Keturah bowed her head.

Eliphaz nodded his assent and responded, "My wife, Keturah." She nodded slowly, her gaze never leaving Channa's face. Keturah's face was expressionless. Only her eyes betrayed her exhaustion.

Channa arose and quietly clapped her hands. A house servant appeared and placed a serving tray of cool mint tea and raisin cakes on a low table in front of the couch. Channa served her guests and family the refreshments. Job and Eliphaz quietly conversed about the weather and the trip.

Seating herself close to Keturah, Channa lightly touched her visitor's arm and spoke softly. "I am pleased you chose to accompany your husband to our home. I trust the accommodations will be to your satisfaction. I look forward to knowing you. And please, call me Channa." With a smile, she sipped from her cup, observing her guest.

A surprised expression crossed Keturah's face. Her eyes widened at her hostess's disarming reception. For the first time in days, she breathed a barely perceptible sigh of relief and shyly returned a smile. Raising her cup to parched lips, she sipped the refreshing tea with gratitude.

Timidly, Keturah surveyed the room around her. The furnishings were comfortable. The walls and tables were tastefully decorated. Channa's daughters were quietly and politely conversing among themselves. Then her eyes found it . . . the lamp in the window.

Keturah glanced at Channa then back to the lamp. Clearing her throat, she softly spoke. "Your lamp is beautiful. I saw the light in your window from many miles away. It was faint at first, but I kept my eyes on it. As we drew closer the flame was more distinctive. It was comforting to know our journey's end was near." She swallowed another sip of tea.

Channa looked at the lamp, her head cocked to one side. She placed her cup on the nearby table. "It is beautiful indeed. I cannot take credit, for it belongs to my dear servant-companion Adah. As a child, she was abandoned in the wilderness. She knows neither who her parents are, nor their reasoning for such a heinous act. But the terror of that near fatal experience has forever seared her conscience. She survived three days of wandering in dangerous terrain, wild animals, hunger and intense thirst in that desert. Near death she saw the hospitality lamp shining for any wayfaring stranger needing shelter, in the window of my parents' home."

Keturah's eyes filled with sympathetic tears. "How unforgivable," she remarked, placing her teacup on the table.

"Yes," Channa replied. "My parents nursed her back to health. Since then she has been, and will always be, my dearest companion. She collects and makes lamps. When possible, she lights one in here every night."

"Is that one bought or handmade?" asked a curious Keturah.

Channa arose and retrieved the flickering light. Tenderly, she placed the lamp in Keturah's hands.

"This lovely lady is named Selah." Channa laughed at the surprised look on Keturah's face. "My Adah thinks it perfectly natural to name her possessions." Once again seating herself, Channa drank her remaining tea as her guest openly admired the lamp.

"You must be fatigued," Job said, rising to his feet. Eliphaz and Keturah nodded agreement.

"Please follow me," Channa said, graciously rising from the couch. She led the way to the spacious and cool guest chamber. Their room was located on the west side of the homestead. The bedroom had a service table of his-and-her washbasins, towels, and a pitcher of well water. Another smaller side table held fresh fruits, nuts, and passion juice. Keturah sank down on the side of the bed, exhausted beyond words.

"I have a bath drawn for you beyond this screen," Channa said, as she stepped to a tastefully designed alcove near the ample windows on the west wall. Just beyond the delicately painted screen, a tub of warm water awaited them.

"I have tried to anticipate your needs and trust you will be comfortable here. Rest well." With a courteous bow, she quietly withdrew from the chamber. As night fell, the household quietly retired from a busy day. Goodnights were exchanged, and most lamps extinguished as a hush settled over the peaceful homestead.

"What do you think of Keturah?" asked Job as he dressed for bed. Channa paused brushing her shoulder length hair and turned to look at him.

"I'm not sure yet, but she seems nervous. I think she needs us." She resumed brushing.

"Mmm," Job replied. "I imagine this trip has been stressful for her. The first year of marriage can be a difficult period of adjustment. Lifestyle changes are inevitable. It sets the foundation for your future together."

Early in their marriage, Job and Channa named their home and its vast territory Shiloh. It became a living memorial to their abiding faith in the Creator God, a deliberate oasis in the land of Uz. All who entered her doors entered a sanctuary of tranquility.

Channa nodded her head in agreement. "My prayer is to encourage her in any way. She is here for a purpose. Time will reveal it. Shiloh has a way of calming anxieties and fears."

As dawn brushed across the eastern sky, the household awoke in stages. Servants began the daily chores. Hundreds of acres of irrigated grasses circled outward from the household. Beyond the perimeters of the trees, men were busily attending the livestock and corrals. House servants addressed the morning needs of the homestead and guests.

The braying of a foal entered the guest room. With sleepy eyes, Keturah lay in the plush bedclothes admiring the luxurious setting. As light slowly penetrated the room, she pushed herself to a half sitting position and viewed the room's furnishings. Light curtains graced wide terrace windows that captured the occasional breeze. The walls were a shade of brown sandstone with hints of red. Heavy cedar wood framed the doorway and generous windows. Thick rugs of deep hues of blues and greens lay near each side of the bed and before the doorway. The large bed had an unusual cover of a deep berry-red made from an incredibly soft material foreign to her. The bed sheets were of the finest Egyptian cotton, the texture silky smooth to touch. Feather pillows of varying sizes completed the ensemble and lay askew upon the floor. A matching sofa with sapphire-colored cushions was near the windows. A small dressing table completed the furnishings. One picture hung on the opposing wall—one rough hand worn with calluses reaching upward, and another hand, unblemished, reaching down in assistance. Simple. Understated. Thought-provoking.

Eliphaz stirred beside her, softly snoring. Their trip had been long and tiring. Rising from the bed, Keturah sank her toes into the thick rug and wiggled them. She then circled the room, caressing each furnishing with unbridled lust. Her husband, a long-time friend and business associate of Job, also arose. A good night's rest had worked wonders for both of them.

A light knock at the door announced the arrival of a servant girl. "Breakfast is ready," she stated quietly and left the couple. Because they were hungry, it did not take them long to dress and join the family.

From the dining room doorway, Eliphaz and Keturah beheld the splendid buffet. An arrangement of fresh apples, bananas, figs, and pomegranates, pastries, cheeses, and nuts decorated the family table. Fruit juices, goats' milk, and boiled eggs were on a nearby serving table. Job, Channa, and their daughters sat around the rectangular table. Two chairs at Job's right hand awaited their honored guests. As soon as Eliphaz and Keturah were seated, Job rose and blessed the meal. The men quietly discussed the business purpose for this visit, oblivious to the ladies.

From across the table, Channa spoke warmly to her guest. "Keturah, today is a day of relaxation for you. Your trip was long and tiring. My home is your home. Please avail yourself of all its comforts." Keturah nodded her gratitude between bites and smiled shyly in response.

Breakfast was unhurried and enjoyable. Snippets of lively conversation between Channa's daughters floated over the table, as they talked and giggled among themselves. Occasionally, Keturah furtively glanced back and forth between the animated girls. Her eyes betrayed her quiet demeanor. She did not join their exchanges, though Channa was certain that all were of similar ages. Keturah was a very young bride, not at all what Channa expected.

Quietly clearing her throat and glancing at her daughters for silence, Channa turned her gaze upon Keturah and said, "I have arranged a trip to the Bazaar in two days, if that is pleasing to you." Channa's eyes twinkled as a smile played about her lips.

Her daughters were delighted to hear the news and choruses of "May we go, too?" filled the room. With raised eyebrows, Job sent a meaningful look toward his rather vocal daughters. Calm was immediately restored. Their question hung heavy in the air. A slow, lazy smile crossed their father's face. He knew how much these trips meant to his offspring.

"Please pass the salt. I can't eat boiled eggs without it," he said as he was carefully peeling off the outer shells. His daughters watched him with bated breath. "How much is this going to cost me?" he teased. All three girls jumped from their seats and ran to their father, joyfully embracing him. The commotion was short-lived as the girls realized they had plans to make. Taking their leave, they quickly exited the room. The sound of their eager voices slowly faded.

Keturah looked hopefully at her husband for his approval. He slightly inclined his head in agreement between bites of fruit. Unconsciously twisting a strand of her hair, she looked timidly at Channa, and then quickly bowed her head. "Thank you," she quietly replied and toyed with the fruit on her plate.

Looking to Eliphaz, Job spoke. "I am glad your trip was uneventful. I have looked forward to this time. Your insight will be of grave importance to the city elders. We have many hours of work before us. These next few weeks we shall travel between here and Bozrah. Today, let us enjoy each other's fine company. Tomorrow we shall leave immediately after breakfast and return in time for dinner."

Once again, Eliphaz inclined his head in agreement.

As early morning light barely touched the horizon, Job and Channa awoke. Rising from sleep, they stretched their muscles. Here and there a moan escaped their lips. "We're getting old," muttered Job bending over to touch his toes with as little effort as possible. Straightening his body, he placed his hands on his hips, shook his head and grimaced at the thought.

Channa stretched her arms heavenward, yawned from deep inside, and then replied, "You, Sweetheart, may be getting old, but I am only maturing." She giggled, her sides shaking at his dour face. Job looked suggestively at her, his right eyebrow slowly lifting as he considered her. He winked. Even after all these years together he still knew how to make her blush and feel like a desirable woman. Washing the remaining sleep from their faces, they poured themselves cups of pomegranate tea. Approaching the eastern windows in time-honed harmony, hand in hand they stepped onto the patio and sat on the settee.

Job was the first to speak. "My dear, did you sleep well?"

"I slept well, my beloved," she replied with a lazy smile and squeezed his hand.

A faint ray of sunlight fell on her raven hair. Job never tired of looking at her, his first and only love. He could not imagine life without her. They had never talked of marriage in their youth; they just instinctively knew they would always be together. So did their parents.

They met when they were eight years old at a festival and became instant soul mates. Their parents were celebrating with other Bozrah citizens, the completion of another cistern midtown. Job's father was a respected elder. His wisdom and fairness were legendary. Job's mother was a quiet woman, content to nurture her many children, grandchildren, and great-grandchildren. Job and his brothers followed their father's example. His oldest brother was a scribe, well versed in the laws of the region. Job, a successful business man, amassed vast land holdings and livestock. He and his sons owned the largest camel enterprise. He was also an elected city magistrate. His younger brother owned the second largest camel import-export business in the territory. Together, these two brothers influenced the regional markets.

Channa's parents were visionaries. They had predicted the growth of Bozrah and the surrounding territories. They used their family holdings to invest in two Inns. Their foresight had encouraged new trade to the area. Channa's mother was also a gifted seamstress and hostess.

Channa inherited her mother's flair for fashion and hospitable graces, which earned her a reputation as a woman of fine taste and kindness. However, her strength of character and gentleness enamored Job. Her beautiful eyes and wonderful smile only enhanced her attractiveness. His integrity and honor had captivated her. With time and determination, they became as one in harmony of thought and actions.

Job looked out at the advancing dawn, a soft sigh escaping his lips. "The Merchants and Traders Guilds weigh heavy on your mind," Channa remarked, sipping on her warm tea.

"Yes. I am glad friend Eliphaz is here to give counsel to the elders. He has witnessed similar challenges from his region. Taxes are the result of all economic growth. The Guilders need the protection of fair laws as they ply their trade. We will broker a compromise between them and the city leaders. Eliphaz's wisdom is to be heard." He finished his drink and sat the cup down, reaching his arm around Channa's shoulders.

From the horizon, prismatic sunbeams pierced the sky. Daybreak unveiled itself in full glory. The coo of a lone dove drifted upon the air as varying hues of color painted the morning sky. "Another masterpiece for us to enjoy. And your day?" he inquired.

Channa chuckled. "I shall call our adventure 'Ladies Day Out.' The girls are so eager to visit Bazaar and have saved up their coins. Keturah is anticipating the adventure herself." Turning to face her husband with eyes wide in amazement, she asked, "Did you know that she has never been to an open market? Imagine that." Job smiled at his beloved and waited for her to continue. "She is a quiet one to be sure. I get the impression she has experienced very little of what we deem normal. Do you know anything about her family?"

Job chuckled softly. "Eliphaz is not an easy man to live with and this marriage was more to his advantage than hers. He overlooks her lack of maturity in the desire for her to bear him a son, an heir. Her family profited from the arrangement . . . he will take care of her."

Channa's forehead furrowed as she digested the information. "Keturah is a young bride and eager to please her husband. I have noticed her submission to him. She is timid but I perceive a teachable spirit. Eliphaz chose well. I plan to treat her to the relaxing mineral waters, as their trip was long and arduous. A little shopping . . . a taste of different cuisines . . . a refreshed wife! A beautiful and rested wife is a great reward for a husband, yes?" Her eyes danced and her dimples framed a most delectable mouth as she teased him.

Job brought her close and kissed her passionately. Murmuring softly against her lips, he replied, "A most exquisite reward indeed."

After a few shared minutes, Job composed himself. "Shall we pray now?"

Lifting their heads from prayer, an explosion of glorious light greeted them as the sun mounted on wings and rose up before them. Morning had arrived.

Over breakfast, Job and Eliphaz had their heads close together discussing their day's schedule. Channa disclosed the carefully planned schedule with the excited women. The air was electric with anticipation! Servants quickly cleared away the last traces of a scantily eaten breakfast. Immediately after the meal, the women donned their finest apparel, bid Job and Eliphaz farewell, and departed post haste for their great adventure!

The double-seated carriage offered very little protection from the dusty road. The women held veils over their faces between conversations. Anticipation was ripe and added to their pleasure. Channa's daughters chatted amiably betwixt themselves, musing over the booths they planned to frequent. The twins, Kelila and Kefira, were eager to explore the open markets of crafts and handiwork. They were of the age to attract the attention of the opposite sex. Channa had "the talk" with them two years previously. *Then* they had looked bored and not sure any changes were on the way. *Now* they knew they were attractive women and enjoyed the admiring glances directed toward them. Channa's eldest daughter, Jamina, planned to stroll through the exotic foods and herbs. A beautiful and graceful young woman, she also had her share of attentions.

"Jamina, did Cook give you a list of cooking herbs and spices?" asked her mother.

"No, Mother, but I know what ingredients she has on hand and can easily compliment them. She does like to experiment on us, doesn't she?" This comment brought a giggle from her sisters.

Leaning forward to hear more easily, Channa spoke to Keturah. "My dear, as this is your first visit to our Bazaar, I want to treat you to the finest we have to offer." With that said, Channa happily settled herself into the comfortable cushions of the family buggy. Disguising her observations, Channa studied her guest.

Keturah sat across from Channa, her bright eyes big as saucers and her enthusiasm barely contained. The Bazaar! She excitedly rubbed her hands together. She had not stopped smiling and giggling all morning! *Of course* Keturah had heard about the marketplace. Who had not? The network of merchants, traders, bankers, and artisans was integral to the expanse and commerce of the region. But to *attend* Bazaar? She had not indulged that thought, *ever!* Being the young bride of an older and settled man, she had resigned herself to a dull, boring, and empty life. When her husband asked if she desired to accompany him on a business trip to the land of Uz, she nearly leaped with joy! Moreover, to be the guests of the distinguished Job and Channa was an honor beyond her imagination! The prospect of meeting Channa was a bit daunting, but curiosity and extreme tedium prompted her decision. Job may be the wisest and wealthiest man in the East, but his wife Channa was the one that women talked about and admired. Keturah needed this opportunity to stimulate her wilting and disappointed spirit. *"Perhaps, just perhaps, Mrs. Job will accept and favor me. Perhaps she will mentor me. Oh, how I need a friend. May this journey transform my life."* This unspoken prayer lay etched on her hungry heart.

A bump in the road brought Keturah's thoughts back to the present. The sounds of the Bazaar were audible now. She leaned her head close to the open window. As they rounded a curve in the road, her breath was taken away at the sheer magnitude of the marketplace. She was not prepared for its size! Tents and displays spread across miles of terrain. She wished she had better sandals.

Upon arrival, Channa's daughters, accompanied by a chaperon, bid their mother and Keturah a fond farewell and were off to their own endeavors. This gave Channa the freedom she desired to introduce Keturah to her preferred luxuries.

The Bazaar was beyond Keturah's imagination. The noise of trade, friendly banter between merchants, and strolling musicians filled the air. Vivid colors, ceaseless activity, and pungent smells attacked the senses. The sheer multitude of people created a massive swell of kinetic energy.

Caravans from as far away as Babylon and Memphis, Ezion-Geber and Carchemish, traversed the known trade routes through Uz. Cargoes of gold from Ophir, topaz from Ethiopia, silver, precious stones, jewels, frankincense, along with exotic, rare spices like cinnamon and nutmeg, overwhelmed the senses.

The city Bozrah was a mecca for apothecaries, artisans, merchants, traders, and academics. The magnet that attracted commerce also invited crime, vices, and corruption. Laws and ordinances were in place to protect the general citizenry and promote commerce and trade. It was toward the promotion of healthy city growth that Job had sent for Eliphaz. To Keturah, these issues were minute; she was going shopping in the largest and most diversified district in the territory, maybe even the world! Moreover, Channa the wife of Job, was her private guide! Could it get any better than this?

Paramount on Channa's "must experience" list was the mineral waters treatment of the highest order, an essential for pampered women! She took Keturah's arm and led her toward a delicately framed doorway, their bodyguard not far behind them.

"Oh, Keturah, I believe every woman needs to treat herself to a luxury when she is tired, frustrated, or in need of celebrating. Don't you?" Before Keturah could reply, attendants whisked them away. The next three hours they splurged in the most incredible beautifying experience known to women. By the time they left, both women felt like beautiful queens as they rejoined the flow of humanity.

Refreshments at the impressive Tea House were next, with delicious aromas tempting their senses. Teas of all flavors from the known world and dainty delicacies to delight the taste buds were abundant.

Their next stop was a visit to the perfumery. Here they inhaled the scents of many compounds, spices, and incenses. They left with many purchases: presents for family and friends, scented candles, and perfumes for themselves.

At the appointed time, they met Channa's daughters and shared a late lunch before going their separate ways again. The afternoon's leisurely stroll through the inner court of the Bazaar allowed them to shop to their hearts' content.

As they strolled through the booths, Keturah noticed how frequently the merchants acknowledged Channa with respectful bows. She addressed many of them by name. It was evident they highly regarded her. She was a noble woman by virtue. She smiled warmly at those around her and had a kind word for all. She was not afraid to touch others; she would rest her hand on the shoulder of a widow and encourage her, or for a harried merchant she would lightly touch an arm and ask after the family. The effect was soothing. Sometimes, a careening child darted through the crowd calling "Mrs. Job, Mrs. Job." Channa would pause and open her arms to happily receive the child. Keturah began to hide within her hungry heart the godly kindheartedness of her hostess.

The day progressed with lots of laughter and camaraderie. A deep friendship was birthed and one lonely heart began to heal. All too soon, it was time to leave.

From the prearranged meeting place near the Bazaar entrance, the five women collected their many treasures and were then escorted to the home of Channa's parents.

There they spent the evening relaxing. Channa listened to Kelila, Kefira, and Jamina as they amusingly entertained their grandparents with the telling of their days' adventure. Keturah, less timid now, joined in the conversation and was introduced to the art of herbal gardening. An early bedtime proved most relaxing to the tired shoppers.

Dawn saw them returning to Shiloh amid new baskets of all sorts and sizes; bolts of fancy and textured fabrics of fine linen, purple and silk and scarlet; bejeweled chains and pendants of gold; and exotic foods. All were pleased with their extravaganza. Ladies Day Out was a huge success!

Much sooner than either Channa or Keturah wanted, the conclusion of the business trip was upon them. Tomorrow, Eliphaz and Keturah would be returning to Tema. Keturah had found a mentor and friend in Channa.

On the eve of their departure, Channa led Keturah arm in arm to the inner courtyard. Seating themselves, they inhaled the fragrance of the fruit trees surrounding them. Keturah steeled herself for the goodbye she knew was coming, but deeply dreaded. She had learned so much from Channa during this visitation. Her hostess had not only become her confidant, but also her heart-sister.

Channa gazed deeply into the approaching twilight. She weighed her words carefully. "My beloved sister Keturah, I discern a deep hunger within you. Wives must learn to love their husbands, and this takes time. Men are a strange lot sometimes. But the Almighty made them that way!" Both women chuckled as they shook their heads in complete agreement.

Channa continued, "How to love Eliphaz—that is the task before you." Channa paused, praying for wisdom. "To love your husband, you must commit yourself to know him: his likes and dislikes, habits and oddities; learn these things well. Eliphaz is older than you are and more experienced in the ways of the world. Trust his judgment. God created men to respond to the respect from their wives, children, and peers. Do not demand Eliphaz's love. Honor him in all you say and do. Let your beauty not be merely outward such as ornaments or fancy clothes, but rather a gentle and quiet spirit. I see these virtues in you. Can you see them?" She turned and looked at Keturah.

The question surprised Keturah. She did not think of herself as endowed with such admirable qualities. Channa laughed at her friend's astonishment and hugged her.

"Yes, yes, you *do* possess these qualities my sister. But," Channa hesitated and looked searingly into Keturah's eyes and ultimately, her soul, "You must faithfully seek the help of the Almighty to nurture and bring to fruition these seeds of Godliness. You cannot do it on your own. No woman can." The words hung heavy in the air between them.

Keturah reached for Channa's hand. She knew she had much to ponder.

"I have a gift for you," said Channa. She reached under her seat and presented a gift box to her friend. Slowly, Keturah unwrapped the contents. In her hands she held a delicate but intricately wrought hospitality lamp. Tears slipped down her cheeks.

"Thank you, my sister. May we pray?" Keturah asked. Kneeling and clasping hands together, they humbly prayed in unison:

> "Creator God, bless me and keep me.
> Let Your face shine upon me.
> Be gracious to me.
> And give me Your peace."

"I have learned so much from you, my dearest friend." Keturah was fighting back the tears as her camel rose from its kneeling position.

"And I from you," replied a misty-eyed Channa, dabbing at her tears.

The camels lumbered into position facing south. Turning in her saddle, Keturah frantically waved her arms and called back over her shoulder as the caravan began walking away, "You will come to visit me, yes? I will leave a light for you!"

"Yes, yes," shouted Channa, waving a final goodbye.

Chapter 2

*Her husband is known in the gates when he sits
among the elders of the land. Proverb 31:23*

"Mistress, the master returns in haste," Adah said breathlessly as she hurried through the doorframe. Her voice and eyes were laced with alarm. Her recovery was almost complete. She still needed rest.

"Have a seat," Channa ordered rising from her chair. She ran through the foyer to the front door. Job was riding hard from the direction of Bozrah, his horse kicking up clouds of dust. He was home early, too early! His position as city elder and judge required him to be in Bozrah every week for two or three days at a time. He had ridden out early yesterday morning and now he was returning? Something was seriously wrong!

His horse halted at the porch. Dismounting, he threw the reins of the perspiring steed to the stable man. Without speaking, he strode past Channa to the inner sanctum of their bedroom. She quickly and nervously followed him. Silently, she closed the door behind herself and leaned against it for support. He paced the floor. Frustration shown in his face. His lips were pencil thin and clamped shut. The agitation in his movements alarmed Channa, causing her to breathe in shallow gasps.

"Have a seat my beloved husband and calm yourself," she managed to utter.

Ignoring her suggestion, Job crossed the room and stared out the window, his hands on his hips. It had been years since she had seen him so shaken. Channa remained still, barely breathing, waiting for him to speak.

Turning to face her, he breathed deeply and spoke. "Channa, the Sabeans are threatening to break the peace treaty. They have sent emissaries to the Chaldeans in hopes of forming a union with them against our city-state. Our elders are discussing the organization of a militia."

At this news, Channa took a seat herself. For more years than anyone remembered, skirmishes and hostilities had rocked the region. Territorial disputes and raids on livestock had been common fare. Establishing a Peace Treaty beneficial to all the region and the addition of the Incense Trade Route had been a dream for many throughout the territory of Uz and its bordering land. Trade routes were around or through some, but not all the territories until twenty years ago. The Peace Treaty had been a hard-won achievement with months of negotiations and multiple compromises. The accepted covenant had established peace throughout the region by having the trade routes pass through each territory, thus ensuring the opportunity for all populations easy access to commerce. Twenty years of hard-won peace and now this possible dissolution!

"But why, Job?" she asked from her side of the room.

"The son of a Sabean duke and a Chaldean man are accused of murdering one of our Bazaar merchants. They were caught red-handed, stealing. When confronted by the merchant, they attacked and murdered him with a sword and injured his wife also."

"Channa," Job came to her reaching for her hands, "the merchant was Abdul. And his wife, your friend, is badly injured."

She gasped as her shoulders sank. Job squeezed her hands. Her face was ashen with shock and tears spilled forth. He dropped to his knees in front of her, his eyes never leaving her face. Tenderly, he brushed a loose strand of hair from her cheek.

"When did it happen? Will she live?" she asked, her thoughts turning toward her friend.

Gently, he wiped the tears on her face and replied, "Five nights ago. Her condition is severe. The healer thinks she will recover with time and diligent care."

Biting her bottom lip, Channa took a few deep breaths trying to regain her composure. "And . . . and the family?"

Still holding her cold hands, he continued, "The family is demanding immediate execution. They have a legal claim for justice and restitution, an eye for an eye, the law of the land. But another is involved, one of our own." Job hesitated, shaking his head. "He is a troublemaker and attracts others so inclined. He was reprimanded by the elders a few years ago and strongly encouraged to leave the city. Obviously he has returned, with new and dangerous friends. Apparently, they are the ones responsible for the escalating thievery amid many of the merchants. This has been a problem for quite some time. Eliphaz was beneficial in establishing the position of liaison between merchants and city elders. This cooperation benefits the city, merchants, and caravan traders for continued economic growth. Last night was the first time these lawbreakers were caught in the act and violence was the end result." Job released her cold hands and sat on the floor. Drawing his knees to his chin, he then wrapped his arms around his legs. "They may have committed other crimes and possibly murders in surrounding regions and fled here. Couriers with accusations of this crime were sent to our allied city-states. Justice will be dealt, but at what cost?" His words hung in the air between them. He rested his weary head upon his knees.

Channa reached out and tenderly stroked his head. He looked up at her with a faint lopsided smile. It wrenched her heart to see him in such turmoil. She searched the face of this honorable man whom she deeply loved. Job had an obligation to judge righteously between the victims and the accused. He would dispense justice for this grieving family, of that she was certain. But there were complications, political ones affecting the city and region. She waited with a heavy heart, her thoughts returning to her now widowed friend.

Job eased away from her and rose to his feet. He returned to the window and view. "The Sabean descends from a long line of the privileged. His father is one of the Sabean dukes who signed the peace treaty twenty years ago. I have observed this young man. He is proud, smug, and unrepentant. Looking into his eyes is like staring into a deep well of evil. I saw no fear of the Almighty or impending judgment." Job shuddered, the memory still fresh. "The Chaldean is also unrepentant, malice lacing his every hateful word. He refuses food, relying on water only."

"What of the Uzzite? Is he repentant? Do we know his family?" Channa asked, wondering at the blatant lack of fear these violent young men had toward the Almighty.

Job took a slow, deep breath then exhaled and turned toward her, his hands clasped behind his back. "The Uzzite, one of us . . . turning upon his own community. No we do not know him or his family. Only his crime and reputation." Job's stooped shoulders and downcast eyes tore at her heart. Minutes passed. Then with tightly clenched hands held high, he angrily cried, "Have we so quickly forgotten the condition of man before the Flood? What have we learned from history?"

His outburst subsiding, he purposefully gathered his thoughts. "The Uzzite is displaying remorse; whether genuine or not, I do not know. His family is openly shunning him. He requested the priest visit him. I pray he is sincere."

Job was deep in thought as he sat next to Channa. She arose, stepping to the door. She clapped her hands and a maid appeared with figs, raisin cakes, and goat's milk. After a brief rest, he continued.

"The accusations will be spoken aloud before the city elders and in the presence of witnesses in two weeks, allowing time for magistrates and family members to arrive for the trial. The right of revenge will be heard. Since they were caught in the very act of murder, they have no defense for innocence. The court is merely a formality and judgment will be swift. My major concern at this point is the security of the city and wisdom to preserve the peace treaty."

They sat in quietness as twilight fell. With heavy-laden hearts, they did what they always did when faced with difficult challenges—they sought the face of Almighty God. Kneeling together, they spent the next several hours deep in prayer and sorrow.

The city of Bozrah was on edge. As Job and Channa rode through the streets, they sensed the tension everywhere. They arrived without incidents at Channa's parental home. It had been decided that she not attend the afternoon trial in case of an uprising. Job left to attend his responsibilities.

During the past two weeks, Bozrah's population had greatly increased. The influx of Sabeans was quite noticeable and alarming to the general citizenry. Sabeans were easily recognizable on the streets, their characteristic height betraying them. Their reputation as rustlers and rough characters preceded them. The presence of multitudes of incoming Chaldeans arrayed in their distinctive flowing vermilion turbans and broad belts had disturbed many of the city leaders. Some feared that these Chaldeans might be magicians or conjurers, there to practice their craft and affect the outcome of the trial proceedings. Dread of more violence and reprisal hung in the air.

The fathers of the accused Sabean and Chaldean prisoners arrived amid groups of armed bodyguards. Refusing accommodations inside the city gates, they pitched their tents outside the wall. Arrangements for visiting the condemned were made. Rumors and suspicions multiplied and circulated freely as tensions increased. Mob violence was a very real threat to these proceedings. Uppermost in the minds of many was the thought, *"will the Peace Treaty be upheld?"*

As a precaution, Job had ordered protectors to patrol the outer gates and placed others in strategic vantage points within the city to forestall any trouble. Magistrates from nearby provinces arrived days before the court convened. Job knew this trial had far-reaching consequences, not only for Bozrah but also for all the territories involved in the Peace Treaty.

As Job walked to the city gates, he grieved over the ugly mood prevalent in this, his city of birth. He silently prayed as he approached the seated tribunal. *"Creator God, forgive us our many sins against You. We are a contrary people, bent on doing our way as opposed to Your righteous way. I need Your guidance today. Help me to serve justice to all those involved, to display kindness instead of anger, and to walk humbly with You and for You."*

Job reached the courtyard, his countenance sad but decisive. Benjamin and Adam, his sons, were waiting and flanked him. Elihu, Job's apprentice, approached and spoke quietly as they walked toward the judgment seat. Nodding his head in affirmation, Job then dismissed his assistant. Crossing the last few steps with his sons beside him, he took his seat. Court was now in session.

The entire proceeding was accomplished by midafternoon. Praying ceaselessly, Channa and her just-as-anxious parents impatiently awaited Job. She paced the length of the cloister many times. Disquieting thoughts filled her heart. Repeated eruptions of angry shouting were audible to them. Frequently twisting her hands in agitation, she was relieved when Job walked into the private secluded garden. Not realizing it, she held her breath at the sight of his pinched face and tense bearing. He approached his waiting loved ones and sat in the closest chair. Channa took a breath and joined him. He was quiet and reflective. Except for the slight tremor of his hand as he reached for hers, he appeared calm. No one spoke. A servant appeared with cool goats' milk and raisin cakes. Absentmindedly, he accepted a cup of milk and slowly drank the refreshment as he collected himself.

Clearing his throat, he began. "It was nasty. I think most of the city's population was there. The witnesses were angry and often furiously interrupted by cries of retribution from the merchants and citizens. The three fathers of the condemned men were seated with the city elders and visiting magistrates, adhering to the covenants of the Peace Treaty. Throughout the trial, the Sabean and Chaldean laughed mockingly, hurling insults and curses at the crowds and magistrates." Job paused, shaking his head, then inhaled deeply.

He continued, "The Uzzite was silent however. He never took his eyes off his father. His father just stood immobile, his head bowed in grief. Unlike the other accused ones, who come from wealth and position, this father has no standing in the community. He is just a hardworking family man. Halfway through the trial, that man began to cry. Slowly he raised his head and looked deep into his son's eyes for the rest of the trial. At sentencing, his son cried out pleading for mercy and forgiveness . . . it fell on the deaf ears of the crowd. When Abdul's family demanded 'an eye for an eye' revenge, the crowd erupted in mad cheers. When I pronounced judgment of immediate execution of the guilty men, I was apprehensive of the reaction of the many Sabeans and Chaldeans, highly visible just beyond the crowd. The Sabean duke arose and tore his robes in anger, yelling at his son. The Chaldean father tore his clothes, spat on the ground and cursed the day his son was born. As the two of them left, so did their fellow countrymen, following them in peace. But the Uzzite father, he . . ." Job could not speak for the raw emotion overwhelming him. Using the back of his hand he wiped the tears away. "This father ran to his condemned son and embraced him. He then fell on his knees, tore his clothes and forgave his son." Job could not stop the cascade of tears. His family quietly wept with him.

The mournful cooing of a dove registered on his mind. Composing himself, he resumed. "The crowd was so unruly by then that few people noticed. The Almighty did. I think that this condemned son was not asking the crowd for mercy and forgiveness, but his father."

Few minutes more and Job fully collected himself. He glanced toward the sun. "The stoning should be over by now. Justice has been served. A life for a life."

He rose from his chair. Looking at the circle of loved ones, he read the sadness in their faces. "Today is a day of grave consequences. Healing for Abdul's family and our city can now begin." Extending his hand to Channa he said, "Let us return home."

Chapter 3

Her children rise up and call her blessed. Proverb 31:28

Channa sat quietly in her patio chair with her feet propped up, cushions comfortably positioned around her. Deep in thought, her gaze concentrated upon the delicate fragrant narcissus flower in her hand. Several yards beyond her, a field of cultivated white narcissus spread their beauty. From time to time, air currents from the plains caused the flowers to ripple in gentle, hypnotic waves. Today the flowers danced.

"Mother, are you busy?" asked Jamina, pausing in the doorway.

Channa looked up at her firstborn daughter. With a mental jolt, she realized almost as if seeing Jamina for the first time, how attractive her daughter had become. She carried herself with quiet confidence and poise, a beautiful warm smile, her greeting to the world. Jamina's demeanor was one of calmness and grace. She was very much like her father, thoughtful and inquisitive, and full of tenacity. Channa thought, *"Oh Job, we have done something right to have such a daughter."*

"No, I am not busy. I have been reflecting on today and its glory. The Almighty has once again created a most magnificent day for our pleasure," she replied, spreading her hands to the wide-open fields beyond them.

Jamina came out to the terrace, pausing shortly to breathe deeply of the wafting scent of sun-drenched narcissus. She sat at her mother's feet, resting her hands and chin on Channa's knees. This was a favorite and confidential position for both of them. They sat in comfortable silence for a few minutes, Channa stroking her daughter's raven hair. She knew to wait; her daughter would speak when she was ready.

Jamina turned her face toward her mother and said, "I watched Keturah during her visit last season. She seemed unsure of herself and almost . . ." She hesitated searching for the exact word, "Fragile. She studied you the entire time she was here. No matter what you did or said, she took note of it. She appeared to be more comfortable with us than with her own husband. Why?"

Channa was very much aware of the intense scrutiny that took place. She smiled at the memory. "So that is what has aroused your curiosity. For starters, Keturah is a very young bride in an arranged marriage to a much older man. As such, she has certain obligations to him first and foremost. Age barriers can be daunting. Keturah has much to learn of the world around her and grow into that knowledge. She left the comforts and customs of the home of her father for an unfamiliar home with Eliphaz. She is now wife of a prominent businessman and mistress of her house. The duties and responsibilities required to transform a household into a home are staggering. It is a task God has well equipped every woman to accomplish. She is now the 'Eve' in her surroundings. Her choices will set the course of not only her future but also her descendants and legacy."

Channa paused as recollections of her early marital days flitted through her mind. A subtle "hmm, hmm" from Jamina brought her thoughts back to the present. Shifting in her chair, she resumed speaking. "Surely, she misses the companionship and freedoms of other young women her age. In addition, Eliphaz is settled in his ways. He has experienced much of life and is content. Now he wants an heir. Keturah has gone from the protection of her father to the protection and demands of a husband. Her dreams are subject to her husband's wishes. Such is the culture we live in. This is a marriage of convenience and secures her financial future, especially if she bears an heir. She will have a comfortable life. Eliphaz is level headed and a fair man. He will provide her creature comforts."

Jamina took a few minutes to mull over her mother's explanation. Then she sat upright, fully facing her mother. Her eyes shone brightly with the depth of emotion emanating from her heart. "Creature comforts, yes, but rightfully so. Mother, what about her dreams? Surely, she has them. You saw how happy she was with us. She is most agreeable and has a smooth type of humor; her giggling fits are contagious! She blossomed in our midst and enjoyed herself. However, when *he* was around, she became quiet and withdrawn. I do not think he even once smiled or praised Keturah the entire time they were here! I feel sorry for her, trapped by tradition in marriage to a boring and unimaginative man. And yes, Mother, he is dull and *booor-ing*. He has been here on three different occasions and the conversation is always the same: long tedious speeches punctuated with 'I have learned, I have experienced, I have seen.'" Jamina grimaced, then closed her eyes and shook her head as if ridding her mind of the remembrances. With her finger, she traced a design on the tiled flooring. Her voice was low. "Mother . . . do you suppose they ever talk about anything important or intimate or just plain silly?" Her sadness and compassion were touching.

Channa was surprised at her daughter's outburst. "I hope so," she replied.

Jamina raised her gaze. "Will you think me too bold if I say he strikes me as a little proud and haughty?" She paused, looked away and then muttered under her breath, "Someone needs to tell him that haughtiness is no perfume."

Channa reprovingly cleared her throat at her daughter's observation. She silently shared the same unfavorable opinion of Keturah's husband.

"What does father see in him?" Jamina inquired.

Channa drank deeply of the sweet-scented air. She lifted the narcissus flower to her face and caressed her cheeks and lips with the soft petals. Softly she replied, "Eliphaz became a business associate of your father before we married. He has aided your father many times in legal situations. In regards to Keturah," she paused and gently touched her daughter's shoulder, "it is her choice if she will have a satisfying life."

"Can her marriage ever be like yours and father's?" Pity laced her voice.

Glancing to the open field, Channa basked in the beauty of the brilliant waves of narcissus. It took time and attention to cultivate them, to nurture them to twenty inches in height, to bring them to full maturity and marketable value. Slowly, she framed her response. "No. Your father and I are close in age. Our philosophy of life and our faith in God are the same. We have the advantage of having grown together as a couple. We have made good and poor decisions in the past and will do so in the future also. We have loved deeply, fought, and reconciled together. Time is a great teacher. Our choice to honor and respect each other is what the Almighty has taught us to do. In our obedience to God, He blesses us as a couple. Keturah and Eliphaz must navigate differences in age and expectations. Eliphaz experienced life as a young energetic man. Keturah has yet to taste the wine of life. They will make their own way and their marriage will reflect their choices. Such is the way with all couples." Channa smiled and her hand tenderly caressed Jamina's upturned face.

"I pray God sends me a godly man just like father. A man that I can admire, respect, and love as you do father. Perhaps that day will not be far away." Jamina sighed and her shoulders drooped. Her furrowed brow tickled her mother.

"Anyone in particular?" Channa asked, teasingly.

Jamina quickly dropped her gaze, but not before her mother saw her flushed cheeks. The telltale signs that Jamina did indeed have a young man in mind. She apparently had been giving it some thought for quite a while! "Oh, Mother," she said a little breathlessly, her attention focused on her clasped hands in her lap. Rising to her feet, she kissed her mother. "Thank you for modeling for us the noble way to honor and respect a husband." Then she was gone, but not before Channa saw a glistening of tears.

Twilight filtered through the windows and filled the bedroom. Job was relaxing against the doorjamb opening onto the patio. His thoughts were elsewhere. Pulling back the coverlet, Channa spoke into his reverie. "I had a most interesting conversation this afternoon with your daughter." She sat on the edge of the bed to get a better look at him.

Turning from the doorway, he stared at her, a slow smile stretching across his face. Lightly folding his arms across his chest he said, "By 'my daughter' you mean Shadow."

Channa gave a slight nod, her smile matching his. Oh, how she loved just looking at him! Now in middle age he was even more attractive to her than ever!

Job cleared his throat and drew her back from her musing. "What about Shadow?"

Shadow was the pet name for Jamina. From her birth, there existed a bond between them beyond description. After having seven sons, Job had begun to wonder if he would have daughters. Then *she* was born. One look into her baby eyes and he was hooked! He had carried her everywhere with him. When she started walking, about the time of her twin sisters' births, she was nicknamed "Shadow" by the household staff. Wherever Job was, she could be found in his shadow, from the camel stockyards to the sheepcotes. After all these years, only Job and a select few of the elderly servants used her nickname. Channa rejoiced over their closeness. They were so alike in temperament and action. He was a great father and loved each of his children deeply. He prayed diligently for all of them and his grandchildren. Their children knew that he loved each of them. Jamina, though, was a carbon copy of her father. Her siblings were not jealous of her, as they were secure in their father's demonstrated love for them. What greater gift could a father give his children?

She recounted most of the earlier conversation between Jamina and herself.

"My daughter is an observant one! Wise . . . like her father," he beamed, his chest puffing outward. He resumed his propping position against the doorpost, perfectly relaxed.

"More than wise," Channa laughed gaily, "she is nudging us."

"Nudging us?" he asked. His right eyebrow rose inquiringly.

"She has grown up, my beloved husband. She is hinting about getting married herself. She is of age."

Standing erect now, Job's forehead furrowed as he began digesting this obviously disturbing news. *They look exactly alike when they are thinking*, she thought. He turned back to the gathering darkness just beyond the door. The full moon was visible. Behind him, Channa lit a lamp. And waited.

"I suppose you are right," he responded. His voice was low and thoughtful.

Stealing to his side, she took his hand in hers looking into the blackness.

He continued, "God richly blesses us with prosperity, friends, good health, and peace. But the greatest blessing is His gift of family to us. I always wanted to be married to a wonderful woman," he paused and looked adoringly into Channa's upturned face, "and have many children."

Channa reached up and tenderly kissed him.

Once again facing the darkness, he continued, "I was so proud when the boys told us they were ready to marry. They are fine men aren't they?"

"Yes, they are beloved, very fine men." More silence. More waiting.

"And they chose godly women who respect and honor them, for wives. And now we have many energetic grandchildren to love," he smiled contentedly.

"And to spoil," Channa interjected. He softly chuckled in agreement.

A light breeze wafted through the air. Job thoughtfully rubbed his chin. "I knew in my mind that this day would come but my heart is not ready to let her go. I just can't imagine her not here with us . . . and riding herd on the twins."

Leaving his side, Channa busied herself around the room. "We are not contemplating sending her to the ends of the earth. Just marriage. To a local boy." Her words sounded hollow to her ears. "**Very** local!" It suddenly hit her that Jamina would be leaving their home, moving out, when she married. Now Channa was disturbed. She seated herself and began unconsciously fidgeting with her hands. "Who do you think are good prospects, worthy of our daughter?" she asked quietly, pushing down the unease threatening to overwhelm her heart.

Job turned around and went to his chair. He was all business now. "I have observed Daniel, apprentice to the scribe Levi. He listens well, is teachable, and works hard at his tasks. You have met him?"

"Yes I know him. But he is boring and tends to gluttony," Channa replied stiffly.

After a few minutes of reflection, Job said grudgingly, "And so he does. What about Joseph? He is from a good family. He cares well for his mother since his father's death and has expanded his land and livestock."

"Yes, my husband, he does. However, his mother is bitter and critical. He stays in the field a lot. Should Jamina marry him, she would have to endure his mother day in and day out. And so-would-we! at every visit." A grimace flashed across her usually peaceful face. Crossing her arms over her chest, she glared at him.

Job tried hard not to laugh at her but failed in his feeble attempt.

"Don't you look at me like that, Job! And stop laughing! This is serious. One does not marry an individual . . . they marry a family! You just might want to be a bit pickier about who we want to be related to!" Her eyes were ablaze and her chin tilted in defiance. Rising from her chair, she paced around the room to calm herself. With difficulty, she took a few deep, cleansing breaths and returned to her seat. Reaching for her hairbrush, she began to brush her long hair.

It took all his might to reign in his amusement over her reaction. "Who do you . . . umm like, Sweetheart?" An innocent smile played on his lips and his voice dripped with honey. She shot a suspicious glance at him.

"What about Luke?" she offered.

Job thought for a few minutes. "He has proven himself a fearless leader and neighbor during some of the occasional raids on the camels."

"He is gentle, patient, and protective with his younger sister although she is slow of wit. In addition, he is a capable overseer of the family livestock. His parents will want for nothing. Admirable qualities," Channa affirmed.

"He listens respectfully to the elders and is honest in all his dealings," Job added.

"My beloved husband, what is most important is his heart. He fears God. With the right woman, he will go far. Do you not agree?" Channa gazed deeply into his eyes, willing herself to see into his very soul.

"I have made my choice. I will seek opportunity to speak with Luke and his father in regards to marrying our daughter." Job smiled smugly at her, quite content with his decision. Channa smiled in return and inclined her head in assent. She knew what Job did not: Jamina herself would be most pleased with this news. She replaced the hairbrush to its tray.

"What are you thinking now, dear wife? Have we forgotten something?"

"Oh . . . just how handsome you are my beloved. Outstanding among ten thousand."

His right eyebrow arched. "Just ten thousand?" he teasingly asked and snuffed the lamp.

Chapter 4

*She makes fine linen garments and sells them, and
delivers sashes to the merchant. Proverb 31:24*

"Ouch! That hurts," yelped Kelila, furiously rubbing her left eyebrow. Lifting her polished bronze hand mirror close to her face, she surveyed the irritated area and groaned at the redness. "Oh, don't be such a whiny baby," retorted Kefira, hands on her hips, barely suppressing her amusement at her twin's reaction. "You now look *chic* with evenly matched eyebrows."

"Am I scarred for life?" asked Kelila, her eyebrows now puffy from the yanking of unwanted brow hair. Kefira was always talking her twin into being a guinea pig whenever there was a new beauty procedure to try.

"Why do you let her talk you into these things, Kelila?" asked Jamina, chuckling as she passed through the door into the spacious workroom.

"*Because* she makes it sound so easy and necessary." Kelila was using her fingers to softly rub her tender eyebrows in a circular motion.

"Because," interjected Kefira in a highly exaggerated tone as she flounced around the room imitating a former tutor, "the advancement of this business is built upon our testing and approving each product and procedure. It is our *duty* to our clientele and we simply *must* validate every procedure." She politely curtsied.

"You mean, experiment with each product and procedure on me!" added Kelila, and they all burst into laughter.

Kefira returned to her sisters' side. "Now if you pull your hair back like this," her hands began to style Kelila's hair, "and make a braided row here . . . look in your mirror and tell me what you think!"

"I think my eyebrows still hurt," Kelila replied ruefully, moving her mirror around her head. "Hmm, I do like the hairstyle. What do you think, Jamina?"

Jamina was absently watching them from the comfort of her desk. Cup in hand, she was enjoying her morning pomegranate tea, the pungent smell wafting to her nose. Her father was the only other person she knew who liked their tea so strong. "I like the stylishness."

"Well, you girls seem to be in high spirits today," greeted Channa as she entered the room. She raised an eyebrow when she saw Kelila's face and instinctively turned to Kefira for an explanation.

Kefira cleared her throat. "Mother, I heard some of the servants talking about the new look on Egyptian women! They are painting colors on their eyelids and shaping their eyebrows. It is supposed to enhance your physical beauty!"

Channa had seated herself and was looking intently between her twins, shaking her head and smiling. Oh, the mischief of her daughters!

"How do I look, Mother?" asked Kelila, glancing between her mother, sisters and her oval mirror.

"Well . . . hmm," Channa looked down at her clasped hands and thought for a minute or two.

"Do you not approve, Mother?" asked Kelila, anxiety lacing her voice.

Kefira walked to her mother and knelt before her, looking earnestly into her face. Channa looked into her daughter's innocent eyes and gently smiled. Lifting her gaze to include all her daughters, she asked, "My dears, I wonder if beauty can be packaged?"

A thoughtful pause filled the room. The sound of bees floated on the breeze outside.

"But, Mother, our business is to make women beautiful," replied Kefira. Kelila nodded her head in agreement.

"Do we make others beautiful or . . . do we help them protect their natural beauty?" Channa questioned.

"I'm not sure I understand the difference," commented Jamina, her brow furrowed in contemplation.

"The moisturizers we make . . . do they really change our appearance? No, but do we not feel more attractive when our skin is smooth and soft? The fragrances we blend into perfumes make us feel special and sweet smelling. You see, we do not sell beauty. We merely enhance what God has created."

"In all honesty," Kefira, never one to mince words, said, "some women do not have a chance for natural beauty." Jamina rolled her eyes and shook her head, suppressing a laugh. Kelila looked away, her hands covering her mouth and her shoulders shaking with silent laughter.

Channa bit her bottom lip to suppress her mirth and took a slow, deep breath. Her daughter's frankness always surprised her. She clasped Kefira's hands and looked into her daughter's upturned face. Prudently, she weighed her next words. "Beauty is in the eyes of the beholder. But for those less blessed physically, as well as those abundantly blessed, I believe the Almighty looks not for external adornments like jewelry, fancy clothes or painted eyes and arched eyebrows," she shot a quick gaze over to Kelila who grimaced, "but rather holiness in the hidden person of the heart. Qualities of a gentle and quiet spirit and submissive and respectful behavior are highly treasured. This, I believe, is what makes a woman truly beautiful. Genuine beauty is more an attitude than an external application."

Rising to her feet, she beamed at her daughters and announced, "Now, barring any more injury," she glanced down meaningfully at Kefira, "we have work to do. The trade route caravans will be arriving in Bozrah within the next four weeks and our beautifiers must be ready for market. The next few weeks will be busy ones. Roll up your sleeves, my girls, we have work to do!"

Everyone went to her designated task. Kelila and Kefira were most creative in the 'mixing and making' aspect of their mother's business. They were great assistants to Channa, especially when developing new products! Their ingenious talent was the nurturing of local and imported flora. A large floral and herbal garden flourished just beyond the workroom walls. No matter the poor condition of any fledgling plant, they intuitively knew how to nurse it back to health. They often sang to their 'babies' in the nursery of plants. Today, their task was pouring and sealing moisturizer and perfumes into clay jars for the coming caravan.

Jamina appreciated numbers and organization. She often assisted her father and brothers with livestock inventory and records. However, in here, she was invaluable to Channa with her knack for accounting and marketing. Her desktop held schedules, orders for merchandise and a map of the caravan routes.

"Father has contracted with the tribe of Jerusha's father to supply us with clay jars for next season's shipment of moisturizers, Mother."

"Good. When can we expect delivery?" asked Channa, placing her hand upon her daughter's shoulder and glancing over the open ledger before them.

"They should be ready within fourteen weeks. That allows us plenty of time to complete this shipment and start on the next one. There were three designs from which to choose. I selected the one with two doves, their wings, like hands, barely touching each other. Knowing that the dove is your favorite bird," she paused and smiled up at her mother, "and you and Father like to hold hands, I propose that we make the doves our business signature."

Kelila and Kefira voiced their approval from the opposite side of the room. Channa glanced in their direction. They were already discussing the importance of having a professional look and personal emblem. *"Oh dear,"* she thought, *"My daughters are more knowledgeable about these sort of things than I."*

"I like that, dear," said Channa, trying to imagine the jars.

Jamina continued, "And, Mother, Father said we need a business name." She resumed her bookkeeping and schedules unaware of her mother's qualms.

Channa approached her workbench with a furrowed brow. "A business signature, a business name, this is getting complicated," she whispered, her voice laced with a tinge of irritation.

This season was the first time she dared venture to export her products outside their region of commerce. Job had arranged transportation and distribution of her beautifiers through a known merchant. This tradesman had international connections and frequently traveled the caravan routes.

Because Channa was known locally, there was no need for a business name while bartering and selling her moisturizers and perfumes in the Bazaar. But now . . . she was going transnational!

She sat at her desk and leaned forward, one arm prostrating on the desktop and the other supporting her chin and cheek. It took effort to collect her scattered thoughts. Job was the one who saw the vision for this expansion. The thought of her products being in the hands of foreigners was a bit daunting. What if no one outside this region liked the moisturizers? Now that could be depressing! But Job had a head for good business. Chewing on a sprig of mint, she sat back in her chair and mulled over possible titles. There was Job and Sons for the camel import/export business their sons managed. What about Channa and Daughters? No, that seemed a bit bold. A woman in business was still frowned upon by many others. Unfortunately, it was still a man's world when it came to business. Thankfully, Job was a man ahead of his times; he recognized and appreciated the contributions women made to the business community.

Channa felt the beginning of a headache. Looking outdoors at the floral garden did nothing to inspire her. Turning to her daughters she announced, "We have a challenge. Your father says we need a company name. I want each of you to deliberate over this important decision and give me your input later." Three heads bobbed up and down in agreement as they continued working.

Channa took a few deep cleansing breaths. *"I'm fine. This is a great opportunity for all of us. I am not alone in this,"* she told herself. *"Job will help and the girls are great assistants! One step at a time, just like when I first began."* Peace returned to her soul. Now she was ready to work. She turned her attention to the recipe box on her desk. Contained inside were formulas and prescriptions yet to be developed. Flipping through the notes, she pulled out the current ointment recipe for care of the feet. Conventional treatment for parched, cracked soles and heels was wax taken from sheep. This lanolin was—at best—yellowish, thick and most unpleasant to smell. Surely, there was a better salve to be made. As a young woman, she observed the ravages of the sun and arid desert heat and wind upon the skin of men and especially, women and children. The available treatments of wax and animal oils had been less than desirable, being more functional than kind to the skin. She determined then to dedicate herself to the advancement of skin protection. Her noble goal was placed on hold when she married Job and bore ten children. After the birth of her twin daughters, those earlier dreams began to resurface and take shape. Now, twenty-five years later, that resolve had blossomed into a thriving business catering to women's delicate skin.

The Incense Trade Route and King's Highway through Uz brought new incense, oils and herbs from faraway places. During the first five years of her business, she sought the most knowledgeable herbalist in the region and spent time learning the secrets and properties of local flora and herbs. Her interest in the benefits of organic gardening led to the development of moisturizers, healing creams, and ointments. Gifted with an ability to discern subtle nuances in scents, she soon began making perfumes. The effectiveness of her skin treatments earned her an excellent reputation among tradesmen, laborers, and farmers. The moisturizers and perfumes for women made her business very profitable. In neighboring regions, her merchandise was beginning to be recognized, largely due to word of mouth of faithful patrons. With the vision of Job and the marketing efforts of Jamina, who knew how far the business might expand! Garnering her wild thoughts, Channa resumed her work.

"What new fragrances for men and women are you envisioning for this upcoming season?" asked Kelila, munching on a cluster of purple grapes during one of their breaks.

Channa looked up from the passion fruit in her hands and smiled.

"Recipe one for women: main scent, almond . . . secondary scents: balsam and rose. Recipe two: main scent almond . . . secondary scents: grape, honeydew and jasmine."

Her daughters were deep in thought for the next few minutes, drawing upon their sensory knowledge of scents.

"I think they will smell pleasant and uplifting, perfect for every occasion," replied Jamina, between sips of pomegranate tea. "I particularly like the fragrance of rose."

"And the new scent for men?" asked Kefira, slowly munching on figs.

"Recipe for men: main scent nutmeg . . . secondary scents ambar and apple blossoms. Ambar and apple create a very masculine aroma combined with the rich, woody scent of nutmeg. The scent of ambar and its properties intrigues me, my daughters. One of the caravan guards, who knows your brother Benjamin, hails from the coast. His mother and sisters live on the shores of an estuary of the Great Sea. They collect raw ambar, a waxy substance found floating on the ocean surface or washed up on the shore. His family refines it and he sells it to innkeepers on the caravan trade routes. The fragrance is a very unique and pleasing aroma and appears to bond well with the apple and almond oil extracts. Experimenting with it, I have determined that not only is it a fine ingredient in perfumes, but it also acts as a healing agent in my foot cream. Slowly heating ambar will soften it but intense heating will make it burn. It is costly, but well worth the price, I think. I intend using it in some of the women's perfumes, too."

Jamina stretched and yawned. "Mother, the scented soaps, how is that project progressing?"

"Not well at all. I may be heating the cypress or sesame seed oil too long or too quickly."

"What about the ratio of ashes to oils?" asked Kefira, lounging on the floor.

"That is the only part I am sure of right now. The roots of soapwort burn down quickly and evenly. When I mix the ashes with olive oil, the consistency is perfect. But the smell is hard to overcome. So I changed to cypress and sesame seed oil. I used the exact same process each time for consistency, altering the oils. But the smell is not fragrant." Channa sighed and leaned back in her chair, arms crossed over her head.

Kelila was looking out the window at the herbal garden, deep in thought. Turning around, she addressed her mother. "Perhaps the soapwort is wrong. We use soapwort to wash the linens because it does not shrink them. Instead of soapwort . . ." she paused, her brow furrowed in deep thought. "Why not try ashes from the pistachio tree? It has a mild odor when cut and may be easier to scent."

"Or cinnamon bark, it has a strong fragrance," interjected Kefira.

"Cinnamon is too costly." Jamina shook her head as she vetoed the suggestion.

Kelila slowly approached her mother, again thinking aloud. "Okay, perhaps it isn't the soapwort but the sesame oil that is the problem. Jojoba oil is great for massages and bonds well with other essential oils. And the fragrance is distinct, but pleasant."

"And we use it as an anti-inflammatory in the foot creme," added Kefira.

"It has a long shelf life. We have a large inventory of it now." Jamina twirled her pencil between her long, slender fingers, her feet propped atop her desk.

"Hmm. That just might work." Channa picked up her unfinished passion fruit and approached the window, her thoughts weighing the idea. "Thank you, dears. Good observations. Break's over, my girls." She remained at the window deep in thought as she finished the fruit. All resumed their work; the deadline was upon them.

The last crate of moisturizers and ointments was in the final stages of shipping preparation. The past few weeks were often tedious, but tonight their work ceased.

"Mother, will you be traveling anytime this year?" asked Kefira, pausing in her work to look at her mother. "I mean for the business, of course." Her face was the picture of innocence but not her words!

"It has been over two years since your last adventure," commented Kelila, crawling about on hands and knees checking filled crates for any damaged goods.

Channa paused in her packing. Hands on hips, she slowly pivoted in place, surveying her surroundings. Empty shelves and packing crates inside and outside their work area attested the hard work just accomplished. A change of scenery may be in order! She enjoyed the challenge of collecting samples and occasionally traveled out of region to collect new, exotic fragrances and plant oils. As befitting her station in life, she was always accompanied by an escort. She was not timid; travel was a pleasure to her. Sometimes Job accompanied her and a few extra days were added to the agenda. Other times she invited her daughters who were always thrilled and ready for a new 'adventure.'

"And do you girls have a specific place I might need to visit? For the business, of course."

Jamina, Kefira and Kelila immediately ceased their tasks and sat comfortably on the edge of a table, facing their mother. Their innocent smiles belied the mischief dancing in their eyes.

Channa slightly tilted her head to the side and narrowed her eyes. "Mind if I have a seat for this?" she asked.

"Oh please, make yourself comfortable, Mother. Want some figs?" Kefira offered her nearly empty bowl of fruit to the others.

Kelila jumped off the table and dashed to the refreshment nook. She returned shortly with a tray of raisin cakes, fruits and goats' milk. Obviously, it was break time.

Kefira was the first to speak. She gushed, "Well, I overheard the house servant telling Adah that she heard that Elath was fabulous! Mother, it has been ever so long since we, I mean, *you*, traveled to the coast. Surely, a visit for the business of course, is well overdue. Don't you think so?" Her thoughts turned southward to the seaport town and a contented smile crossed her face.

Channa surveyed her daughters. It had been a full season for them all. The two-month visit of Eliphaz and Keturah, the new markets for their cottage industry, and the upcoming family visit had kept them busy.

"I think you are absolutely correct. I shall speak to your father about this matter. A trip to the coast, for business purposes of course," Channa made a wry face which sent her daughters into fits of giggling, "is most appropriate. And of course, for an adventure of this magnitude, I shall need three assistants." The girls hopped from the table, cheering with joy. Grabbing each other's hands, they encircled their mother and began dancing and singing with gusto. The loving looks on their faces would be a vivid memory for her for years to come.

Chapter 5

> So that this man was the greatest of all
> the people of the East. Job 1:3

Sounds from the kitchen signaled the beginnings of breakfast. Job and Channa were on the front porch, pomegranate tea in hand, anticipating the day before them. On the horizon, two small images appeared. Within minutes, riders atop horses were discernible: their firstborn son Benjamin and grandson Josiah. They closed the distance quickly, son racing father. It was a tie at the corral. Alighting from their saddles, they left their mounts in the hands of a servant and hailed Job and Channa as they approached.

After kissing his mother, Benjamin sat on the ground and leaned back against a supporting porch column, stretching out his long legs. Hands clasped behind his head, he asked, "Are the others here?" and yawned deeply.

"You are the first to arrive," replied Job with a small yawn.

Josiah, stretched out full length on the floor near Job, asked, "Grandfather, is breakfast ready?" and yawned with closed eyes.

"Breakfast will be served soon," replied Job, yawning again!

"Like fathers, like sons," Channa said with a snicker. The men ignored her observation.

They relaxed in comfortable silence watching the sun peak over the horizon as it began its circuit in the skies. Soon the noise of many approaching horses and lighthearted jesting heralded the arrival of the other six sons of Job and Channa. The boisterous men dismounted and came to the house, greeting the rest of the family. Each son leaned down and lovingly kissed their mother on her upturned cheeks. "Time to eat?" someone asked.

Breakfast was a noisy affair. The brothers exchanged the latest happenings of their families and homesteads. With their father Job, they discussed the current market values and the bi-annual livestock review. The men would leave after breakfast and be gone for six weeks as they inventoried the sheep, camels, oxen and donkeys grazing throughout their properties. It was a mammoth responsibility but necessary. The Round Up was the preparation for the marketplaces, camal caravans, and sheep and cattle drives. In addition, the rotation of the grazing lands needed reviewed. Their vast livestock and lands required routine assessments.

Job and Channa had never taken lightly the wealth with which God blessed them. They taught their children "to whom much is given, much will be required." This year marked the first outing for Josiah, their firstborn grandson. Now at twelve years, he was to begin his training in the responsibilities of the family business.

"*How quickly they grow up!*" Channa thought to herself as she gazed lovingly at her grandson. In great contentment, she watched the interaction between her "boys." She was proud of all her sons. In their own unique ways, each one contributed to the smooth and successful operation of the family enterprises. Every one of them had built a homestead when they married and now each one had children. Benjamin was a lawyer and kept everything current and legal. Jobe, Boaz and Noah were full-time ranchers, preferring the great outdoors as their occupation. Adam was the scribe in the family. Like his father and eldest brother, he spent time in Bozrah where his skills were in great demand. Enoch was the manager of the family's camel export business. Under his brilliant leadership, Job and Sons became the largest distributor of camels in the region. Jared was the shepherd with his gentle and quiet ways. He also was the gifted musician and entertained the family at special celebrations. "*Truly,*" she thought to herself, "*we have been greatly favored by the Almighty.*"

Breakfast concluded amid much revelry.

Provisions for their trip were awaiting the cargo camels. This was the men's domain and Channa quietly mused as she watched the preparations. Jamal, a most experienced camel driver, was directing the camels. With his staff, he lightly tapped the well-calloused right knee of Siroc, lead camel, and the huge beast slowly bent its front legs and dropped to its knees, the tough, leathery skin pads acting as cushions. Then it folded its hind legs and sank to the ground. Jamal repeated the process camel to camel, until there was a yard full of the kneeling creatures. The sight always fascinated Channa. These giant beasts of burden were bowing to the will of man. Quickly, they were loaded with foods, tents, luxuries and that most precious commodity, water.

Jamal once again took command and one by one, he directed the camels to straighten their hind legs. Then with a jerk, each one unfolded their front legs and rose to heights of six to seven feet. These amazing creatures themselves could easily weigh in at 1600 pounds, not adding their cargo weight! She knew personally of many camels that had been in their herds for almost 50 years. Seeing Josiah dangerously darting in and out through the camels, she quickly called him to her side. "Watch very carefully. Camels are skittish creatures; you must respect their nature. Do you see Ajax? He is irritating some of them. And they will react."

Inevitably, one of the younger servant boys would unthinkingly go near an irritated camel, capable of kicking its legs in all four directions, and be soundly booted or spat upon. Today was no exception. Ajax was warned, but he did not heed it. He ran too close to the head of an older camel and was kicked and sent sprawling in the dirt, yelping in severe pain!

Channa quickly turned away and ran smack into Job's chest. She hid her face in his shirt and tried to contain her laughter, but her heaving shoulders gave her away. This always solicited a laugh from her, as well as the others, no matter the victim. It was always so sudden and comical. And so predictable.

Job leaned down and whispered in her ear, "I do believe, my beloved wife, that you derive a sadistic pleasure from this," while barely concealing his own laughter! Regaining her composure, she once again faced the scene before her. Josiah was bent over his knees, laughing, as was the entire company. Ajax, helped by Jobe, was limping from the scene, more embarrassed than injured. Seeing his mother's quizzical look, Jobe shook his head "No" affirming Ajax had no serious injury.

She was careful herself to give wide berth to any camel. Before the arrival of grandchildren, it was her privilege to join the caravan to the first encampment. Job or one of her sons rode alongside and conversed with her. She learned many lessons on the trail about the greatness of God and creation. Sometimes now, she missed those days. However, a new tradition had replaced that one. It was now customary for all the womenfolk, grandchildren and their personal servants in attendance, to stay with Channa during this six-week period. This time was spent replenishing wardrobes, exchanging recipes and celebrating family.

As part of this new tradition, her daughters chose to spend the week leading up to Family Vacation with their grandparents in Bozrah until the men were gone and their families arrived at Shiloh. Once the little ones arrived, quiet and solitude were at a premium! Twice yearly, the men on Round Up attended the family business and endured being away from their families. They slept on hard ground not far from noisy animals, ate pot luck meals, and infrequently bathed. Meanwhile, Channa and the rest of the family endured sewing, cooking, "creating," and chasing children. Plans were already afoot for the arrival of her sons' families on the following morning.

Josiah took her hand, pulling her thoughts back to the present. "Grandmother, Father has been teaching me about camels." Josiah beamed at her. Recovered from his laughing fit, he was once more fully engrossed in watching the camels and their drivers. "Did you know that camels can run, in short distances, as fast as horses? And that their long, bushy eyelashes protect their eyes and keep the sand out, especially in sandstorms?" She nodded and smiled at him. He continued, "And baby camels are born without a hump! They must look rather silly next to their mammas with their humps. And if a camel is starving, his hump can slip off his back and hang down on its side! Wouldn't you like to see that? I would!" The amazement in his voice tickled her and they both laughed. "Father says that the Almighty must have laughed the day He created them!"

Just then Job joined them and rumpling Josiah's hair, he said, "Jamal wants to know if you are ready to learn how to lead a camel train?" Josiah's eyes were big as saucers.

"May I, Grandfather?"

"My blessing will come with your father's." Josiah disappeared into the crowd, seeking his father.

"Husband, he is so eager to learn the ways of animals and their proper care. May all our grandchildren be astute seekers of the natural abilities granted them by the Almighty."

Job placed his arm across her shoulders. "Time will tell, my dear. Their different talents must be encouraged. I do believe that Josiah will become a diligent herdsman. As for his brother . . . Jobab enjoys "doctoring" the sick. Did you hear of the potion he made for one of the herdsmen's sons? The boy was suffering from upset stomach and Jobab concocted something from herbs he found that eased the pain. We have very intelligent grandchildren."

"Of course, my dear," Channa nodded her agreement. "Look who their grandparents are!" They fell into a contented silence as the last of the preparations were completed. The caravan of cargo camels lumbered toward the horizon. Their sons straddled their individual camels. Servants handed each of the men water bags, satchels of dried fruits, and sweet breads for the journey. At the first encampment, Job and his sons would transfer to horses for the duration of the inventory. The camels were base camp. Josiah was exuberant! His infectious delight touched each of his relatives and laughter was abundant.

Bidding their mother a last farewell, their sons looked on with content to witness Job tenderly embrace and kiss Channa. He searched every inch of her face, memorizing it afresh. "You are altogether beautiful, my most precious one, and there is no blemish in you. How beautiful is our love, my bride."

Her eyes filling with tears, she whispered, "How handsome you are my beloved. Like a cedar tree from Lebanon among the trees of the forest, so is my beloved among the young men. Hurry, my beloved, and be like a gazelle or a young stag and return to me."

Kissing her again, he released her, turned and mounted his camel. Amid much waving and shouted goodbyes, the men headed east.

As they disappeared over the horizon, Channa went inside her house. The quietness was unsettling. It seemed so empty now. Glancing around the room, she felt suddenly alone. Taking a deep breath, she went to her bedroom and fell to her knees. "Oh, God, how empty my world is without my dearly beloved. Protect and guide his every step. And open the eyes of Josiah to see You in new and magnificent ways. May he grow to become a mighty man, just like his father and grandfather. Protect all my sons and use them as You so choose. They are Your children, on loan to Job and I. Thank You for the privilege to parent and love them." Leaving her prayer in the hands of the Almighty, she rose to her feet.

Adah appeared, unbidden, at her side and grasped her hand. "I have a luxurious bath prepared for you . . . perhaps you care to soak until your hands began to shrivel? Afterwards, I think a massage is in order."

"Oh, Adah, you know me so well. How blessed I am to have you! I think you read my mind better than I do." Channa felt the loneliness lifting. Tomorrow and for the next six weeks, she would be a grandmother. But *today*, she basked in the praise of her beloved. *Today*, she was the "altogether beautiful" Mrs. Job.

Chapter 6

She looks well to the ways of her household . . . Proverb 31:27

Channa awoke with the dawn, eager to begin the day. She relished these weeks of togetherness. Looking out her window, she prayed, *"Oh God, bless our home with laughter and harmony. May we never take You for granted."*

After a hasty early breakfast, she swept through each of her rooms, inspecting them one last time. "Adah, have all the bedchambers been aired?"

"Yes, mistress," Adah replied with a smile and dutifully followed her from room to room.

"And there are plenty of spare linens for the grandchildren's pallets?"

"Yes, mistress." Adah followed her into the kitchen.

Turning to her kitchen maids, Channa inquired, "Is there plenty of fresh fruits on the tables and in the pantry?"

"Yes mistress, just as you directed," came their reply.

"The children will be here soon. Plenty of raisin cakes and goats' milk for them?" They nodded in affirmation. Channa left the kitchen for the living room inspection. Adah and the maids followed her.

"What have I forgotten?" she mused, her fingers patting her cheeks. Turning full circle, she surveyed her surroundings. "Flowers! Are there garden-fresh flowers in each of the bedrooms?"

Adah lightly touched Channa's arm. Shaking her head and laughing at her mistress' nervousness, she replied, "Everything is ready. We just need them to come."

Closing her eyes, Channa took a deep, calming breath. Smiling in appreciation at her servants, she nodded her head. Adah and the maids withdrew, giggling as they did so.

Suddenly in the distance, the precious sound of children's laughter and singing was heard. Racing to the door, Channa saw several wagons approaching, filled with adults, squirming children, and nursemaids eager to disembark! Her heart sang with joy at the sight of them. Men servants were close by waiting to assist. By the time the families arrived, bodies of all sizes began spilling from every side of the wagons and running in all directions. Two little freight trains came barreling toward her. She braced herself for impact!

"Ganmaw, Ganmaw, we here ta see you!" exclaimed three-year-old identical twins as they squeezed her legs. Bending down, she smothered each of them in kisses and hugs. Their mother was not far behind with their baby sister clasped securely in her arms. By the time everyone had hugged and kissed, refreshments were awaiting them. Mothers spent the next few hours directing the unloading and placement of their family trunks, then organizing and settling their possessions into assigned rooms and closets.

Channa took charge of the grandchildren, leading them and their nursemaids to the play garden. She announced, "My darlings, Grandfather has a surprise for you," and pointed to the newest construction. The children ran to it. Channa sat in one of the many rocking chairs in the courtyard and watched their excitement. Job had spent hours building a "rain shower." He tapped into the irrigation system supplying the homestead. From there he ran a conduit to a hollowed out tree suspended above a portion of the playground. Holes of varying diameters were bored into the newly created reservoir. Upon command, the control valve freed the water. The ensuing effect was a refreshing waterfall. The children ran in and out yelling with joy.

A soft sigh behind her announced the arrival of a daughter-in-love with eleven-month old Olivia hanging from her hip. Channa gladly opened her arms for the yawning baby deposited into her care. Nestling into her grandmothers' neck, the infant was soon sleeping peacefully. Her mama went back to unpacking.

Quietly, Channa rocked and watched the others play. Occasionally, a grandchild appeared, tiptoed up to her and whispered questions into her ears. "What makes ice?" "What her was doing?" "I lub you."

Other times the grandchildren shared their imaginative stories: "And then they flied away; the chickie-chickie-hi-flied-away!" "And they tak-ed it fom me, Ganmaw." She was content and prayed. *"Thank You, God, for blessing me with such wonderful and loving grandchildren. Thank You that their parents love and worship You. These little ones are most precious to You also. Guard their hearts and minds. Uphold them with Your everlasting arms."*

Not far away, one of the toddlers was singing in a lovely monotone as she twirled and danced. Serenity's mama eased into one of the rockers. "Oh Mother, I must tell you what happened last week," she said in a quiet voice. "After most meals, Serenity thrusts her arms into the air, whoops out loud like an overzealous crane and pins me with a look that says, 'You wouldn't dare disappoint someone this adorable, would you?' I step toward the serving table as the flailing and the whooping continues and return with a bowl of fig bits for her tray. As soon as she grasps one, she smiles, coos, and promptly stuffs it into her mouth. Imagine my surprise when, that morning, she did not eat her beloved figs. Not at first. We went through our usual routine. However, that time when her chubby hand reached for the fig, she moved it not toward her mouth but mine instead.. 'You want Mama to eat it?' I asked her. The tiny fist clutching the fig inched closer to my mouth. I opened wide and gladly accepted her selfless gift. She did this at every meal that day. Now she shares her food with anyone around. I am so proud of her."

As if on cue, Serenity stretched her tiny arms and legs, her eyes opening slowly. Channa gazed into the pure innocence lying in her arms. "Are you ready to go to Mama?"

Late afternoon sun began to cast its shadow from the sundial. "I beat you! You didn't saw me and I beat you!" crowed five-year-old Cayenne panting as she draped herself across Channa's lap. She was playing hide-and-seek with her cousins and Grandmother was the neutral zone. "Mimi, I lost another tooth!" Opening her mouth wide, she proudly pointed to a vacant spot.

"My goodness. Did it hurt?" Channa surveyed the sight.

"No. It came out in the apple. Love you. Bye!" Running as fast as her legs could carry her, she rejoined the game.

Mothers appeared and began claiming children for the evening meal.

Channa's daughters arrived in time for supper. Evening settled over the full household, slowly winding down from its busyness. Children were hugged, kissed and put to bed. The womenfolk gathered on the front porch, talking over cups of variously flavored teas. As darkness fell, each one retired to her quarters for a good night's rest.

It was midmorning and time for a break. Much of the sewing was completed. Grandchildren were happily playing together. Mothers were on the porch, taste testing a new recipe. "I really like this drink. What is the recipe?" asked Jamina.

"One or two sprigs of mint, two or three dollops of honey and cool water to taste," replied Elizabeth. "I have added a splash of pomegranate or mulberry before but prefer it this way."

"I think I will try that myself," replied Channa. "Father likes pomegranates."

"I have been experimenting with the sweetbread recipe you gave me last year, Mother, and I am pleased with the results," interjected Lilith. "I have been adding nuts and mulberries to it. The children think they are on holiday when I prepare it," she giggled. The others joined in with more recipes and cooking triumphs and disasters!

Channa unobtrusively observed each of her daughters-in-love. She had chosen early in her role as mother-in-law to love and accept these women as her own daughters. Many of her contemporaries experienced bad relationships with the spouses of their children. She deliberately called them her daughters-in-*love* because she chose to love them. She and Job had diligently prayed for the future mates of each of their children from their births. The Almighty had blessed those prayers.

Rising from her seat, she stepped away from the group. Looking out to the play garden, she saw Samara, a most tenacious three-year-old. She had climbed every obstacle she could find during this visit, causing Channa some concern. Channa watched with bated breath as Samara reached for the lowest branches of a nearby myrtle tree. A voice spoke softly behind her shoulder.

"Amazing, isn't she? She seems to fear nothing. I worry she will fall and break her leg, arm or neck! I cannot keep her from climbing. My prayer life has intensified since birthing her! Daily I pray for her safety. I pray more for her than the other three put together. I do what I can and leave the rest in God's hands." Jerusha's eyes never left her adventurous daughter. Then Channa noticed the nursemaid not far from Samara. She suddenly realized that the nanny was always ever-present. Turning around, she smiled as she hugged her daughter-in-love.

"You are a good mother, Jerusha. And a wise one, too."

"Thank you. I just have one request, Mother; *please* do not let Father transplant any large cedars from the coast until after Samara is grown!" Channa and Jerusha exchanged knowing looks and interlocked their arms in agreement.

It was time for the men to return and families to go home. At midmorning, a messenger arrived with news from Job.

"Well, my daughters, this is our last lunch together," announced Channa. "Our men will arrive early tomorrow morning." Grateful cheers burst forth from the women.

"Evening meal will be somewhat rushed with final packing. So let us relish this last afternoon together." She did not know she spoke prophetically.

Clapping her hands, maidservants appeared with a most delicious meal. Conversation centered on completion of last-minute packing details. Quietly, servants cleared the table and refilled drinks. Adah appeared bearing gifts, placing one before each woman. "Oohs" and "aahs" filled the air as the presents were opened.

"Oh, Mother, is this your newest fragrance? The one for men? You create the grandest fragrances in the world!" Jerusha closed her eyes and inhaled the rich scent with satisfaction.

"Umm. It smells woodsy, spicy, and most alluring. What are the ingredients?"

"Sandalwood, myrrh, and frankincense," replied Channa with a satisfied smile.

"But isn't myrrh an aphrodisiac?" asked Lilith as she sniffed her bottle of cologne.

"Definitely!" gushed Jerusha. "Just wait until I put this on my man!"

Her comment and tone of voice caused Jamina and the twins to blush. The married women just laughed amiably at their temporary discomfort.

"Mother, you know I adore this color. This azure blue necklace and ring will go perfectly with my new dress!" breathed Kelila, delicately fingering the jewelry. Looking up at her mother, she asked, "You bought this at bazaar, but . . . how did you know?"

Channa smiled conspiratorially and replied, "A little birdie told me."

Another voice piped in, "Apricots! I saw them at Bazaar on our last trip. Aren't they new imports from the latest trade caravans? Do you eat them raw, with the skin, or roast them?"

Kefira rose to her full stature. With a deadpan expression on her face and arm movements to enhance the effect, she intoned, "Peel the skin off . . . take out the seed . . . open mouth . . . put fresh apricot inside . . . move jaw up and down until apricot is easy to swallow . . . let slide down your throat until it hits your stomach . . . repeat for best results." The room erupted in uproarious laughter!

"Anyone have a recipe for them?" someone asked from the end of the table.

"When buying them, feel them. They must be a little soft. Use them as they are, fresh and uncooked like other fruit. I substituted one-half the amount of apricots for raisins in my almond cake recipe. And it tastes ooh-la-la delicious," responded Lilith, kissing her fingertips for emphasis.

Channa cleared her throat for their attention. "My beloved daughters," she began, looking into the eyes of each one of them, "I have relished our every moment together. Words cannot describe the joy you bring to my life. Thank you. Now, as we prepare for tomorrow, this is my desire for each of you. May wisdom, patience, and forgiveness be a graceful garland to your head and ornaments around your neck." Channa rose to her feet and extended her hands. All arose and clasped their hands together. In unison, they recited:

"Creator God, bless me and keep me.
Let Your face shine upon me.
Be gracious to me.
And give me Your peace."

Lunch was a delightful ending to their family celebration.

The afternoon passed with busy mothers collecting their treasures and belongings in preparation for tomorrows' departures. Wives and children were eager to receive husbands and fathers. It was time to return to their individual homes. Messengers carried announcements to each homestead of the family's return.

The sun was at its highest point. Job and Channa hugged every grandchild at least twice. Jamina, Kefira and Kelila embraced each child and parent one last time. Exhausted sons, daughters-in-love and grandchildren climbed into their respective wagons. As soon as the last group was out of earshot, a dusty and weary Job placed his arm across Channa's shoulders and said, "I am glad to be home. Where is my bath?"

Interrupting him, his daughters said, "Welcome home, Father," hugged him and then made their way into the house.

Chuckling softly, Channa rested her head against his strong, dirty shoulder. Turning him around, they walked toward the door. "By the time you get out of the bath, your bed will be ready. How I have missed you, my beloved."

"And I, you." He lightly squeezed her shoulder. "Do I warrant a massage, fair lady?"

A teasing smile played across her face.

"We'll see . . ." He fell into a most sound sleep as soon as his head touched the pillow.

Chapter 7

Morning light filled the room. Channa surveyed the clothes upon the bed. What else needed packing? In early evening, she and Job were to join the rest of their family for the last two days of their son Benjamin's birthday celebration. Earlier, Job had hinted that perhaps they might not return directly home from the birthday party. "Where might my beloved be taking us?" she wondered aloud, pausing, her face puckered in concentration. Shrugging her shoulders, she smiled contentedly and continued packing.

The season's last northern bound camel caravan had come and gone. Job and Enoch leased hundreds of camels to local businessmen for transporting merchandise to foreign markets. They also hand delivered hundreds more contracted camels to owners up and down the King's Highway through designated caravan inns. Cattle, oxen, donkeys, and sheep were counted and culled. Their livestock was in different holding locations awaiting eastern bound caravans for export markets.

Channa also had a stake in the camel caravans. The new containers Jamina ordered arrived earlier than expected. An additional batch of lotions, perfumes and healing balms were on their way to yet another foreign destination. Four arduous weeks of concentrated effort were now history for her expanding beautifying products. Job had the foresight and experience to multiply her distribution network. In addition, Jamina was now officially the business manager of Lady Shiloh Essentials! The more they tried to explain the ledgers and inventory, projected profit margins and losses, et cetera, et cetera, the more perplexed she became! It all sounded Babylonian to her. Channa knew her strengths, and business management was certainly *not* one of them. The Incense Trade Route was the "baby step" for her export commercial interests. The gargantuan task was only possible because of the family's support. Dear, wise Job, business connoisseur that he was, patiently addressed her every qualm in this bold endeavor.

Indeed, between Job and Jamina, the commercial aspect for this business was in competent hands. She was most thankful for the immense contributions of all her daughters and their individual talents.

With business demands behind her for a full season, she was ready to devote herself to other pursuits.

The packing nearly complete, she picked up her journal of papyri atop the bedside table. Opening the outside door wide, she sat in her thinking chair. Fragrant smells from the open fields drifted through the slowly moving air. Off in the far distance were groves of apple and pomegranate trees. On the west wing of the homestead, Cook was busy prepping her garden for planting of beans, lentils, cucumbers, leeks, and onions. Jamina had bought new seeds at the Bazaar for Cook. It was anyone's guess what new recipes may appear for future meals.

This was the week of her firstborn son's birthday. By family tradition, the entire week was dedicated to family and celebrating. Looking in her journal, she read:

> *Yesterday, we were relaxing in the flower garden; grandchildren were napping or playing. Jerusha told us Benjamin's birthday plan. The first part of birthday week, all the brothers shall construct a new donkey corral. Last year . . . wasn't it a well? No matter. Then the games begin. Jerusha made us pledge to keep secret The Master Plan. We all nodded in agreement, eager to be privy to such top-secret information. "Upon completion of the corral, there is to be a competition," she said. "Oh, really?" someone (I'm not sure who) commented. The others joined in mock surprise, rolling their eyes or smirking in feigned disbelief. Ignoring their sisterly teasing, Jerusha continued, "Ben has designed an*

obstacle course for the race-of-all-races! Each brother must choose an animal from the barn as his means of racing." She paused dramatically, and then cut her mischievous eyes to each of us in the room. I was puzzled. What was she not telling us? Of course! Ben was the one stocking the barn! Knowing my sons' competitive spirits, and that birthdays are for competition, I knew the choices would not be the typical, garden-variety expectations. *"What is he putting in the barn?"* asked Kelila, suspiciously eyeballing her sister-in-love. By now, Jerusha could hardly contain herself. She sat rocking back and forth, holding her laughter in by covering her mouth with her hands. Irrepressibly she blurted out, *"He has ordered a shipment of eight ostriches to arrive one week in advance of the party! Can you imagine the spectacle we shall witness firsthand?"* Near hysteria filled the room. One of the girls fell off her chair, she was laughing so hard! The mental images this revelation evoked was enough to keep us laughing for more than two hours! We all have observed ostriches and their unusual behaviors at Bazaar. This race is going to be outrageous! Today, Lilith, leaving breakfast, flapped her arms like wings and hissed like an ostrich. When we giggled, the little ones began to act the same. I suspect, for the duration of our time, we shall hear a lot of hissing, flapping and probably spitting. Later, Jerusha confided to me that the eighth ostrich is for Job. This is the grand surprise for the rest of the family. I can hardly wait to see my dignified husband astride an ostrich! Benjamin is definitely "raising the bar" for future birthday celebrations!*

Today, Job and I leave to join the birthday celebration. Packing is nearly complete. I look forward to being with our children and grandchildren again. I want to see the pyramids. Many tell me it is worth the journey.

Channa drew a small pyramid on the page and then closed her journal, smiling at the memory. Just beyond the wide doorway and to the east of their room, rose a knoll. Small spirals of smoke rose heavenward, individual burnt offerings for each of their children. She saw Job, his arms uplifted to God, worship as he prayed for each of their children by name.

She turned her gaze from the sacred ritual. Lifting her face and hands in adoration, she prayed, *"Oh God, may all of our sons and daughters walk as closely to You as their godly father walks. Guard their hearts from idols."*

The task of packing was finished. Soon she would have her little ones in her arms again. The great race would be on the last celebration day. Only then would Job be informed that he, too, had an ostrich to race! Surely, Josiah would deliver on his promise to share his adventures from the family the Round Up. Humming a new tune she learned from one of her granddaughters, she lay on the bed for a brief nap, anticipating the birthday celebration.

The afternoon sun cast a shadow on the sundial. Job was attending to last-minute details and instructions with his trusted house servant.

Channa was in the bedchamber completing the last embroidered butterfly on a baby blanket. Unaware of the commotion outside, she was startled when Adah burst into the room, terror causing her voice to shriek. "Mistress, it's master Job! He's . . ."

Before the sentence was completed, Channa sprang from her seated position and raced to the front porch. She halted abruptly at the drama unfolding before her. Dread gripped her heart. Three stock men stood before Job, their clothes caked with sweat and dust. Weeping uncontrollably, they began sinking to their knees, one after another. Wails of deep sorrow, torn from shattered hearts, pierced the still air and rose heavenward. Job's shoulders were stooped and heaving, his head slightly shaking from side to side.

Taking a step toward him, Channa saw him collapse to his knees as he cried out in gut-wrenching sobs, "My God! My God!" His hands clutched his head; he rocked back and forth as wave after wave of sorrow overwhelmed him.

Time was suspended. In slow motion, Channa blinked, trying to absorb the agony before her. She watched spellbound as Job began to tear his clothes in shreds. Moans of agony escaped his lips. Shoulders still heaving, he reached for handfuls of dirt and unsteadily poured them over his bowed head. He prostrated his body on the hard ground, head on his arms, his crying unabated.

"*My beloved, I'm coming!*" she thought, but the words were trapped inside her constricted throat. Her feet froze to the ground, unresponsive to her need to reach Job. *"Am I breathing? Why won't my feet move? Job? Oh God, help me! Please!"*

The trance was broken. With her heart in her mouth, she raced to Job's side.

"Job! Job, my beloved." She flung herself down beside his heaving body. Cradling his head between her hands, she gently turned his tear-drenched face toward her, anxiously searching for understanding. With the baby blanket still clutched in her hand, she tried to wipe his face. Slowly rising to his knees, he grasped her to his chest and began rocking her in his strong arms.

"Channa. Oh, Channa. They're gone. They're all gone. Our children are dead."

Chapter 8

The LORD gave and the LORD has taken away. Job 1:21

Channa sat sideways at her dressing table, vacant eyes staring back at her from her reflection. Dimly, she was aware of movements around her. Someone was addressing her. It was a massive effort on her part to concentrate and make sense of the noise.

"Channa, my child, please look at me! Please." Ever so tenderly, gentle hands cupped her chin and slowly drew her face around to the soft voice. It was her mother, kneeling in front of her, the tears of deep grief flowing freely down her face.

Stroking Channa's cheek, she haltingly spoke, "My darling, this is the hardest thing you will ever have to do. We must," her voice broke and she sagged back on her heels and gasped several deep breaths before continuing. "We must commit your children into the hands of the Almighty. Channa, do you understand me? Job is waiting for us. Channa, we have to go now. It is time." Rising from her knees, she gently pulled Channa to her feet also.

Dazed, Channa allowed her mother to guide her to the front entrance where Job was standing, hands clasped behind his back. He was gazing into the distance. Hearing their approach, he turned to watch them. Channa did not take her eyes off of him; Job, her hero, the man who always stood so tall and confident. But not today; his shoulders were stooped and his head lowered in grief. He mutely reached for her hand and together they left their home to bury their family on the knoll.

The funeral was brief with family members only in attendance. There were so many bodies to bury. Job and Channa's fathers and brothers lowered the children and grandchildren into the ground.

Job ceremonially shaved his head. Then tearing his robe, he fell to his knees with bowed head and lifted his hands heavenward in sorrow. His voice resonated with intense emotion as he falteringly prayed. *"Naked I came from my mother's womb and naked I shall return there."* A loud sob caused him to stop. Woodenly, Channa knelt beside him, her hands clasped over her breaking heart. Their tears mixed together in the dust.

With great effort, Job continued, *"The Lord gave and . . ."* another sob shook his body. *"And the Lord has taken away."* His voice cracked as heaving sobs once again racked his body.

Channa's wails filled the air. Wrapping his strong arms around her, Job haltingly ended his prayer. *"Blessed be the name of the Lord."*

The date trees beyond her bedroom enclosure heavily scented the air. Channa stood rigidly near the patio doorway, her eyes eastward to the knoll where hours before she buried her children and grandchildren. She tightly crossed her arms over her bosom. She felt an invisible wall surrounding her, slowly closing in on her, forcing out the very air in her lungs. Her eyes closed in concentration. *"When did I breathe last?"* she wondered. *"How long can a person live and not take a breath? Breathe, Channa, breathe!"* She forced herself to gulp in the fruity air.

Turning away from the view of the cemetery, she entered the cooler recesses of their home. She was bone weary. A persistent throbbing in her head was slowly intensifying. Her fingertips gently massaged her temples. The funeral preparations of the last week had been emotionally overwhelming. Her sisters and sisters-in-law had shouldered much of the necessary arrangements.

"I must remember to thank them," she muttered to herself. Sometime. Soon. Not now. The throbbing increased.

Her mother entered the room carrying a tray of cool goat's milk, fruits and raisin cakes. Sitting it on the side table, she approached her grieving daughter.

"Another headache? Shall I get a damp cloth for you?" She placed a loving arm around Channa's shoulder.

"No, thank you, Mother. I . . . I shall be fine. Really." Channa tried to smile convincingly.

Her mother gently stroked Channa's cheek. "My darling," she paused, lips trembling.

Taking a deep steadying breath, she continued, "The family has left. Adah has prepared this tray for you. We are all worried about your health. Please try to eat something."

Channa glanced at the tray. The throbs in her head were intensifying. With eyes barely open, she cried out. "Oh, Mother, I am so exhausted. My head aches. My soul aches. My heart . . . ?" she paused and took a deep, jagged breath. "My heart is shredded into a billion pieces." Her voice trailed off. Silent tears coursed down her face.

"And the thought of food . . ." She closed her eyes as if to ward off an evil. One hand instinctively touched her stomach. Dizziness caused her to sway slightly.

Her mother led her to the bedpost for support. "Just a moment dear and you can rest." Quickly, she pulled back the sheets and fluffed the pillows.

Channa resumed rubbing her temples. "Where is Job?" Her words were barely audible.

Her mother looked up from the preparations. Channa's pale face alarmed her. "He is with your father. Let's get you to bed, dear one." Facing Channa, she pushed the long, raven hair behind her shoulders and looked worriedly into her daughter's face. Dark circles were underneath once bright eyes and her cheeks were sunken from grief-induced weight loss.

Channa stepped back from her mother. Placing her hands over her heart, she wailed, "No mother should have to bury her children. And not all of them at the same time! O God, will my heart ever heal? I cannot bear this searing pain as my heart is shredded within me!"

She collapsed to the floor, her grief so intense, washing over her in relentless, unending waves. Only the veil of unconsciousness brought relief.

That sound. What was it? So far away . . .

It was closer now. She struggled to identify that sound. There it was again! Calling out to her, enticing her to consciousness. She fought the fogginess, willing her eyes to open, to respond to the insistent words beckoning to her.

A gentle voice. She recognized that voice! It was softly penetrating her subconscious.

"God . . . give my beloved the consolation she needs in her mother's heart."

The voice was growing stronger, gently summoning her.

"Only You can ease the overwhelming sorrow that we carry. Walk with Channa through this dark and unknown valley of the shadow of death. Oh, God, I need her." The voice broke, sorrow overtaking the speaker. Deeply, he engulfed breaths of air.

"Please lift her up, Lord Almighty. Grant her Your peace, the peace and comfort that passes all understanding. We need You, God, oh, how we need You." Job lay his tear-stained face on the bed beside her. He was kneeling, his grief once more assailing him.

Channa, fully conscious now, reached for him and together they wept for their families, which were no longer.

Chapter 9

The heart of her husband trusts in her. Proverb 31:11

Channa sat on the garden bench in the gathering dusk, her energy spent. It was exactly four weeks since the funeral. The house behind her was quiet, deathly quiet. Her attention was held captive by two rabbits within the play garden boundary. They scampered about, easily startled by the occasional breeze or sudden sounds. Unbidden, a memory—of Jamina chasing a rabbit when she was just two years of age—surfaced. She had chased the poor, terrified rabbit until it scampered out of reach into the nearby field. Jamina cried at his escape and crawled into Channa's lap, babbling about "Where go it?" and not understanding the terror she had inflicted upon the poor rabbit!

The memory brought a faint smile to Channa's face.

Job appeared through the doorway and dropped a kiss upon her head before lowering himself beside her. She handed him some refreshing herbal tea.

"A barley corn for your thoughts," he said gratefully accepting the drink. He watched her closely. A light breeze lifted a strand of her hair. Unconsciously, she tucked it behind her ear.

"Just reminiscing." Her voice was barely audible.

"Care to share?" Job asked. He drained his cup and sat it on the ground.

She shook her head. Sometimes, the emotions were still too raw. She turned, fully facing him, and looked up into his worried eyes. Lifting a hand to his mouth, she traced the outline of his lips. Her fingers then traveled upward to his forehead. Cupping his head in her hands, she delicately kissed him.

Smiling halfheartedly at him, she said, "My love, I think you have acquired a few wrinkles," and rested her head upon his shoulder. Instinctively, he wrapped his arms around her.

"I agree," he murmured into her hair. "Do they make me look more mature and ruggedly handsome?" He pulled away from her and posed.

Narrowing her eyes, she looked at him. "I suppose so. But don't let it go to your head!"

It was good to hear her tease. Job knew his wife. She was a strong woman, rising to every challenge presented to her. She was struggling with her grief and loss and needed time to make sense of it all.

"You did not eat well tonight, my wife." He reached for her hand. Idly, he traced patterns upon her palm.

"I am not hungry."

He took a deep breath, exhaling slowly. He needed divine wisdom.

"I worry for your health."

She offered no response.

Job hesitated. "The cedar trees from the coast have arrived. I forgot about them, what with . . . well, our present circumstances." He glanced at her. She nodded her head. "I think it best to sell them, save but one. It is a strong sapling. If you are agreeable, I want to transplant it to the crest of the knoll tomorrow as a symbol of life to shade our loved ones. What do you think?" He fell silent.

With crystal clarity, she remembered the last intimate conversation with her daughter-in-love Jerusha. "Did I tell you about my last conversation . . . ," she halted, fighting for control of her emotions. Her arms tightly embraced her bosom. Breathing deeply and slowly, she relaxed.

Job waited patiently on her, not knowing what to do to ease her pain.

"During their last visit, Samara climbed everything in sight! Trees, fences, even trellises. She even tried to climb your shower fall." A small giggle escaped her half-smiling lips.

"I was needlessly worried for her safety. Then I realized their nursemaid was never far from Sam at any time. Well . . . Jerusha was concerned that you might transplant large trees closer to the house. Which of course Samara would try to climb them. She asked me to tell you *please wait* until Samara was grown. It was funny . . . then." Channa wiped some tears from her cheek.

"Do you suppose our Samara is climbing trees with the Lord?" Her voice wavered.

Job prayed fervently for wisdom. Clearing his tightened throat, he answered.

"I think that if God put it in her heart to climb trees here, then surely it is okay to climb trees with Him there. He made the trees for our use. He walked and talked with Adam and Eve in the Garden of Eden. He walked and talked with Enoch and Noah. God knows the hearts of His own. Whether they are adventurous little three-year-old children," he paused, a wave of fresh grief washing over him, "or sorrowing grandparents."

Somewhere in the dark a lamb bleated plaintively. Stars sparkled in the canopy of space.

Looking up to the night sky, Channa traced the outline of a constellation with her finger.

"Remember teaching the boys the Great Bear, Orion, the Pleiades and the hidden constellations of the south?" Her hand rested on his.

"Umm. And each of them asked the same question."

In unison they quoted, "Why do I need to know this?" They broke into brief laughter at the precious shared memory.

"As I recall, the twins never did learn them."

"They did not try," Channa said in their defense. "However, they had memorized the names of every eligible young man within the territory!" She chuckled at the recollection and the surprised look on his face. He crossed his arms on his chest.

"Really?" His brows furrowed together as he digested this fresh revelation of his youngest daughters. He imagined he heard the tinkling of their laughter on the breeze. It comforted him.

"Oh, beloved, girls just don't think like boys." She squeezed his hand.

"I think the tree is a most thoughtful memorial to our children. I know they would approve. And I promise to start eating again, for your sake. I need you, Job, oh, how I need you." Her voice broke into quiet sobs. He held her close, his tears intermingling with hers.

"And I need you, beloved," he whispered into the nightfall.

Job and Channa were at a crossroads. Their finances were devastated. Drastic decisions were needed. Adah cleared breakfast from the table and returned with cups of tea. Job set armfuls of leather records and scrolls before them.

"Are you sure you are up to this?" Job asked, looking Channa directly in the eyes.

She swallowed hard, but her eyes never wavered. "Yes."

Job stood in the middle of the room. Out of habit, he placed hands on his hips and tightly pinched his lips. Channa smiled at the sight of him, deep in thought. When the children were little and wanted something, they knew *not* to catch him in this stance. Memories . . . most times they were painful, too fresh. But sometimes like now, they felt good.

Job turned to face her. "I think we need to separate each of the businesses and household inventories. We will have a better understanding of the resources left us."

Channa nodded in agreement. They started from different ends of the table and worked toward each other. Progress was slow at first, but soon Channa recognized distinguishing terminology of each enterprise and more quickly separated them.

Adah appeared in the doorway, "Are you ready for lunch? You have been at this all morning!" Job and Channa looked up in surprise. Someone's tummy growled.

"Yes," they both chimed.

Job spoke carefully, his back to her as he looked out the window at the late afternoon sun. "Our situation is critical."

Channa sat motionless at the table. "Job, look at me." He turned from the window and approached her. She stood and pulled his face close to hers. "I know what you are doing." His eyes avoided hers. "Look at me my beloved. You are trying to protect me from the pain. And for that, I dearly love you." She smiled and tenderly stroked his cheek. "But . . . you can't. I do not expect it of you. We have to walk this valley of sorrow. But we shall emerge together."

She stepped away from him and sat down. "Now, tell me everything, bad, worse, unimaginable. You have sheltered me from the truth long enough."

Job leaned against the table, arms across his chest. Taking a deep breath, he began, "Sabeans rustled the herds of oxen and donkeys grazing in the upper pastures. They chased down and brutally murdered the stock-hands. Only Seth, who delivered the report, survived."

Channa nodded, tears slipping down her face.

Job pulled a chair in front of her, seated himself on the edge of it, and clasped her hands. "All the sheep flocks were herded into the southern valley in preparation of the seasonal market. Every shepherd we had was attending them. A phenomenal storm suddenly erupted. Bolts of lightning exploded and utterly consumed every living thing. Nothing remains but charred ground. *In all my life*, I have never seen anything like it." He arose and strode toward the window again, hands rubbing hair away from his furrowed forehead. His voice dropped lower, almost to a whisper. "Even the *dirt* was seared. It was just acres and acres of scorched ground." He shook his head at the still vivid, but incredulous memory.

Channa watched as her husband sought to understand it all. She gave up trying to make sense of anything last week. It was too painful to contemplate.

Job turned to face her. "We lost all but one very terrified shepherd. He called it 'the fire of God fallen from heaven.'"

"Do I know him?" she asked.

"No. He was newly hired by Jared."

At the mention of her son's name, Channa involuntarily gasped, her hands clenching the chair's armrests. Seeing Job's concern, she forced a small smile. A deep breath released the tension in her. "Jared was our shepherd. Oh, how he loved sheep. I'm fine now. Really. Proceed please."

Job sat on the floor near her, propping his back against a doorjamb. "Three separate bands of marauding Chaldeans hijacked the camel flocks headed for rotational grazing. They murdered all but one of the drivers." He fell silent. The enormity of their losses was overwhelming. Left unspoken was their greatest loss . . . their children.

It took a few minutes before Channa was able to speak. "Were . . . were these attacks retaliation for the trial you presided over in Bozrah?"

Job drew in another deep breath and exhaled slowly. "I have wondered that myself so often. I have begged God for answers, but He is silent." The desire, the overwhelming need to understand a reason for their tragedies plagued both their souls.

In the background, Channa heard preparations for the evening meal. Somewhere in the house, a servant was humming a soft tune. She looked down at her shaking hands. Her thoughts were racing wildly through her head. She lifted downcast eyes and caught Job staring at her. "*He needs me to be strong,*" she thought. "*Oh, God, help me help him.*"

A slow smile crossed her face. "My beloved, may we continue this discussion tomorrow?" she asked. "We have much to ponder. And it is time to eat. I know for a fact that Cook is preparing your favorite meal."

Job slowly rose to his feet and stretched his tense muscles. Reaching out to Channa, he took her hands and pulled her to her feet. "Yes, my love. It is time to relax and enjoy the evening."

Job and Channa were comfortably seated on their patio, tea in hand, watching the sunrise.

"So, you're saying we have no livestock. None to sell or for breeding?" she asked.

"Correct," Job answered.

"What about our emergency fund?" Channa turned to face him, eyes wide with apprehension.

Job leaned forward in his chair, elbows on knees, and stared at the ground. "There is enough in it to supply our basic needs for a year." He leaned back in his chair and looked at her. "But not enough for servants or reseeding or stock." His face was grim; the most severe looking she ever knew it to be.

"What can we do? You must have a plan, Job. This is your strength."

"I was awake half the night praying for wisdom and direction. I believe we have a responsibility to the families of the servants and stockmen killed in the raids and whirlwind. I keep thinking about how I would feel if their fates were visited upon us. Many of them have families. Now, there are widows and orphans in need of help."

Channa closed her eyes. *"Oh, God, I have been so wrapped up in my own grief that I have not thought of these others and their grief. Forgive me,"* she silently prayed. She returned her attention to her husband. "You have avoided telling me the number of servants killed at Benjamin's house." Her voice was monotone, her emotions carefully controlled.

Job hesitated briefly. "The servants and stock men pitched in together and bought Benjamin a saddle for his birthday. He called all of them into the house to thank them. The whirlwind hit during that time. The whole house collapsed on them." Job bowed his head in his hands.

"Breathe, Channa, breathe," she told herself. With her hands, she covered her quivering lips. *"Breathe, just breathe."* She concentrated on the clouds drifting overhead.

From around the homestead came a sound of flapping wings. The heavy thud of webbed feet announced the arrival of "Daisy." She silently meandered just beyond the fringe of the porch, the distinctive pouch under her beak swaying in rhythm to her walk. The Dalmatian pelican belonged to Kelila. The huge bird was now nearly six-feet-tall. Its curly nape feathers, gray legs, and silvery-white plumage were in stark contrast to the irrigated grasslands behind the pet bird.

"Beloved, Kelila's pelican joins us. How much do you think she weighs now?"

Job also watched Daisy. "Her bill is probably a good sixteen inches by now. Perhaps thirty pounds?" he mused. "She's a long ways from her nest. Wonder what brings her here?"

"I hope it's not mating season! Those guttural sounds make me want to scratch my throat. And the barks, hisses and grunts remind me of mad spitting camels," Channa said, unconsciously rubbing her throat.

Job chuckled. "No, it's not mating season. I'll have one of the stockmen return her to the nesting area. I never understood why Kelila wanted a pelican. Do you know?" he asked.

"Hmm, not really. I once overheard her say that she and Daisy were kindred spirits, whatever that means. Remember the time she put that outrageous thing she called a hat on Daisy's head? I thought I would never stop laughing!" By this time Channa and Job were laughing so loudly that Daisy took offense and walked away.

Taking a deep breath, Channa said, "I needed a good laugh. Oh Job, laughter doesn't live in our house anymore." Her wistful expression pricked Job's heart.

"Laughter and joy will return, my love. I promise." He squeezed her hand. "I promise."

"Let me get us some tea and fruits. Then we can continue our discussion," said Channa.

Job stood and clasped his hands behind him. "The one resource we have in abundance is land. Our focus must be to rebuild. It's not like we haven't done this before, right my love?" Channa smiled and nodded in agreement. He continued. "We can grant land allotments to the survivors of servants and stock men. The widows can sell or farm the land. Our obligation to them will be served. As for the remainder of stockmen here, they are faithful workers. I hate to lose them, but we cannot keep them. With recommendations, they should find work quickly. Next, we need to prepare for planting season. Family members have volunteered all necessary seed when the time arrives. Laborers will be needed for planting and harvesting.

I can barter their services at harvest in exchange for a portion of the crops. But for planting season . . . I'm still working on that one. This will cut into our profits of course. Nevertheless, it is a beginning. As for breeding stock . . ." His glum voice tapered off. Job sat down. "My love, we cannot afford household servants for a while." His shoulders drooped, heavy with the weight of their world on them.

"What lands are to be the allotments? What if the widows decide to sell?" asked Channa.

"The most logical choice is the homesteads of Benjamin and Adam. Because of their frequent work in Bozrah, the boys deliberately choose acreage nearest the city. We can recess our property lines, leaving the boundaries unbroken. If these outer lands are sold, it will not impact us."

Channa could not speak; many memories were assailing her senses. "*Breathe, breathe.*"

A breeze danced through the not too distant fields.

Channa arose. "I shall return shortly," she said.

Soon, she returned carrying a small pouch. She pulled her chair directly in front of Job. With a small smile she began. "I, too, spent a lot of time thinking last night. Here are my thoughts. Mother can always use more house servants at the inns. I will send the household servants to her. Cook is getting old. So let's retire her." Channa put her hand into the pouch and pulled out a beautiful unmounted diamond Job had given her. "No objections please. Cook can sell this and retire in style. That leaves Adah."

"There is no way Adah will ever leave you, my love." Job stroked her cheek.

"No, but let's retire her anyway. I think I want her moved into the bedroom across from us." Channa halted and looked away, swallowing a lump in her throat.

Job continued to stroke her. "I know Jamina would be pleased to have Adah in her room."

Channa nodded her head. Taking another deep breath, she continued. "And now for livestock. When the time is right we have these." From her pouch she poured forth sapphires and diamonds collected through the years. "It isn't much. I know these are not polished and refined, but surely they have some value. And the girl's jewelry; this azure blue necklace was costly at Bazaar. This gold ring weighs half a shekel and the gold bracelet weighs five shekels. I am not impressed with such, but our daughters were." She tenderly caressed the pieces in her lap. "Besides, who will wear them now?" Tears again welled up in her eyes.

Job leaned forward and with one hand, he tilted her face up to his. The tears overflowed. He tenderly wiped them away. "I thank God every day for you. I cannot live without you." Pulling her to her feet and into his arms, he held her tightly until the tears stopped.

Job strode into the sitting room. Several days had passed since making their decisions. Channa was humming a tune and surrounded by pieces of material and sewing patterns on the floor. She turned to him with a smile. "I have a surprise for you," he said and sat on the couch.

"Hello, to you, too," she chirped. She left her sewing and sat on his lap.

"Oh. Sorry. How is your day? I have a surprise for you." A smug smile played on his face.

"Okay, what is it?"

He deliberately took his time to answer, adjusting and readjusting the pillows near him.

"Are you comfortable now?" Channa asked in feigned concern.

"Hmm, I think so. What does a man have to do around here to merit a kiss from the lady of the house?"

Channa placed her arms around his neck and leaned in close to him. Her eyes dancing, she whispered, "For you, my ruggedly handsome husband, just pucker up. Are you ready to neck?" It was a quite a while before Channa knew her surprise.

Job was trying to comb his mussed hair. Channa was trying hard to keep a straight face.

He cleared his throat. "I met with the remaining hired hands today. They are pleased that my brothers are willing to hire them and that I shall highly recommend those men going elsewhere. As I left the corral, Zerah, remember him? Approached me with a proposal.

He is a widower. He married late in life and has two daughters. He has no dowry for them. Moreover, his daughters need training for marriage. He wants to stay on and work for us. Permanently. In exchange for his services, he asks the use of the building adjacent to the corrals for housing and access to the food gardens to support the three of them. He offered the services of his daughters as house servants in exchange for tutoring and help in preparing their dowries. With this barter, I now have help. And you, my beloved, have house servants again."

Channa smiled. It was a good solution for them. "Isn't he the one who helped Cook tend the gardens?"

Job nodded.

"When will the girls begin?"

"Tomorrow morning. They are moving into the tack room even as we speak. Is my hair straight?" he asked.

Their evening meal was simple fare: fruits, nuts, raisin cake, and mint tea. Job still refused pomegranate tea, Shadow's favorite. Adah seated herself with them. Their once large family was now three members. Conversation centered on the adjustments each one was making. Job worried about leaving Channa to assume his judicial obligations. She surmised as much.

"I have been thinking, Job. It is time for you to return to your responsibilities in Bozrah." She knew she caught him off guard and smiled at his surprised look. She reached for grapes.

"The thought has crossed my mind." He leaned back in his seat after taking some grapes from her cluster. He winked at her when she started to object.

"Beloved, we all need to establish new routines. Tomorrow, I shall have house servants. Dear Adah is here to personally assist me and train the daughters of Zerah. We are making plans ourselves for redecorating. We don't need you looking over our shoulders. Why not leave tomorrow?"

Job took a bite of cake as he considered the possibility. "I need to pack some clothes."

"I already did it," said Adah, replenishing her plate with more fruit.

"Your father and mother need notified," Job said.

Channa looked at him; she enjoyed looking at him.

"On their last visit I told them to expect you at the first of the lunar cycle." Channa winked and smiled innocently at him. She then busied herself with more grapes.

"Well, it seems you ladies are eager to be rid of me. Then, to Bozrah I shall go. Pass the mint tea, please."

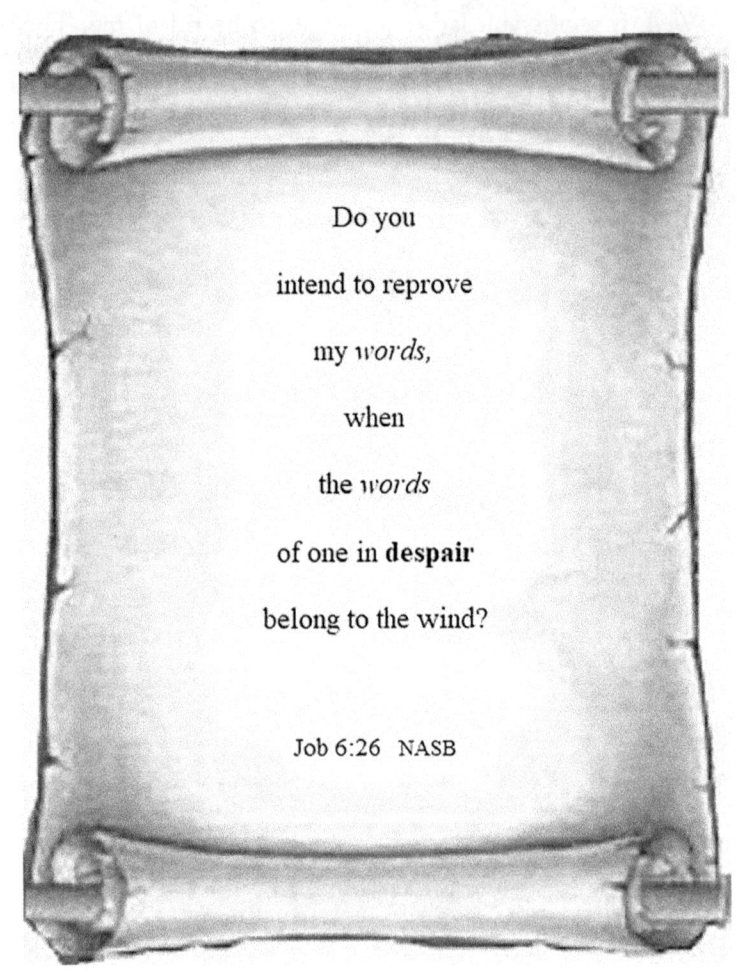

Do you

intend to reprove

my *words*,

when

the *words*

of one in **despair**

belong to the wind?

Job 6:26 NASB

Chapter 10

> She does him good and not harm all the
> days of her life. Proverb 31:12

Channa stood staring, yet unseeing, out the patio doorway. Four months had passed and still Job's illness raged uncontrollably. A soft footfall alerted her to the presence of Adah. "Have you prepared his meal? And a fresh change of clothing and ointments?" Her voice was monotone and devoid of any emotion.

Adah looked up from the breakfast tray she was carrying and surveyed her mistress. Without answering, she placed the food on the table beside Channa's chair. "Please sit and eat your breakfast, my sister. I have brought you fresh pressed jujube tea. The sweet smell still lingers on my hands." Her brow was furrowed; she was profoundly worried about Channa's declining health.

The depression was escalating. Daily, Channa sat in abject silence and darkness for long periods of time. The circles beneath her eyes were more pronounced. Her weight loss was alarming. The absence of Job was taking its toll on her physically and emotionally. She refused any visitors. This past week she became more withdrawn, spending inordinate amounts of time in bed. As weak as she was, she continued the daily trek to deliver fresh food and necessary supplies to Job. No amount of cajoling had swayed her from her mission. She needed to see him, hear him, to know he was still alive.

Slowly turning from the doorway, Channa reached for Adah's hands and raised them to her nose. Closing her eyes, she inhaled deeply the sweet fragrance of jujube. A shadow of a smile played around her lips. She opened her eyes. "My dear sister-friend, always thinking of others." With a gentle squeeze, she released Adah's hands and seated herself. "Breakfast looks good; I shall try to eat. Have master Job's meals ready within the hour. And make sure my buggy has more pillows."

Adah nodded her head in silent compliance and exited the room. *"Oh, God,"* she whispered under her breath, *"Please heal master Job and mistress Channa. Please bring the master home. She needs him."*

Gathering her light shawl closer to her bosom, Channa followed Zerah to the buggy. In his arms was a basket of prepared foods, fruits and water. A cloth pouch held personal toiletries and more ointments for Job. Zerah deposited them on the seat and floorboards and then held Channa's hand as she stepped into the small horse-drawn buggy. He passed her the reins and stepped back. His daughters joined them for last-minute instructions.

"Zerah, have you completed the irrigation inspection and repairs? Master Job is waiting on that report."

Zerah nodded his head and spoke. "The inspection is complete, Mrs. Job. There was a fracture in the lines from the kitchen's outer wall to the well house. I repaired it."

"Thank you. I will return with more instructions." He nodded again and walked away.

Channa looked at the servant girls. "Today is wash day, all household linens." They mutely bobbed their heads and turned back toward the house. Holding hands in sisterly love, they chattered quietly but gaily as they crossed the few feet to the porch and entered the doorway. Channa tilted her head to the side as a memory flashed before her. *"They act and sound just like my girls did,"* she thought. Sadly she forced herself back to the grueling task at hand.

Beams of light from the rising sun pierced the sky. As Channa began the tedious journey to Bozrah's garbage dump, she reflected upon the stifling "sameness" surrounding her. The scenery was the same. The weather was the same. The black mourning clothes were the same. The grief was the same. The overhead buggy canvas, providing shade from the direct rays of the sun, was the same. Smiling ruefully, she contemplated the loneliness surrounding her. *"This time last year I was a very happy and contented wife and mother. My beloved* and strong husband was a well-respected businessman and city elder. Our family . . ." She caught a sob before it escaped her lips.

"Breathe, just breathe," she told herself, intentionally relaxing tense facial and shoulder muscles. After a few minutes of deep breathing, she reached inside one of the baskets and pulled out some figs. The hint of a smile appeared as she savored the rich, sweet taste. "God, I am indeed grateful for this delicious fruit, whether fresh, dried or in cakes," she whispered. "And for the fig trees growing around my home whose large leaves and spreading branches provide us with excellent shade. And to think that this small delectable, created by You for us, is good for eating, fragrances and healing poultices. Healing. Almighty, please spare my beloved. Please heal him. Please."

The miles slowly passed. In her soul, she carefully rehearsed the well-versed words for her meeting with Job. From a distance, the braying of a lone donkey broke the stillness surrounding her. Startled, Channa jerked erect and instinctively pulled on the reins. The horse halted. With lowered head, he snorted in protest and pawed the dirt. Rising to full height, he whinnied and shook his beautiful chestnut mane, awaiting her command.

Shaking her head vigorously, Channa moved uncomfortably on the seat. With one hand free of the reins, she readjusted the pillows. The predictable and monotonous ride was lulling her into a hypnotic half-sleep. Job had cautioned her about this danger. With a flip of the reins, the trip resumed.

"I once had color in my life," she told the horse. "Vibrant colors of many hues, the colors of the rainbow and sky, and colors of the seasons. Now it seems as if everything is either neutral or drab." She looked down at her dreary mourning clothes and wrinkled her nose in disgust. "Or black!" Her shrill voice was steadily climbing in volume and intensity. "How is anyone supposed to survive death or illness when surrounded by so much black?" By now she was yelling. "And just why am I talking to a horse?" The horse tossed his head up and down, ears pricked, neighing as if in sympathy.

Channa wiped tears from her eyes. Silently, her thoughts reflected the emptiness in her heart. "*All remains the same . . . nothing changes.*"

The rhythmic trotting of the horse produced an almost hypnotic effect with the odious refrain. *"All the same, nothing changes. All the same, nothing changes."*

"God, where are You? Why do You allow the torment of my beloved and me? Where are You?" she screamed. The heavens were brass. The hopeless refrain continued, piercing her soul.

It took mental fortitude and sheer will power for Job to move his fatigued and gaunt body from one heap of ashes to another. All day and every day, citizens of Bozrah deposited their household garbage, waste, and human excrement. Fires constantly burned the refuse heaps and a thick, haze drifted upon the stale air.

Job made it a point to come to the outer boundary to meet Channa. The repugnant stench of burning rubbish and decaying animal carcasses covered with maggots always caused her stomach to roil. As always, he swallowed bitter complaints, determined to present to his beloved a cheerful and encouraging countenance. He watched as she stepped down from the wagon and gathered the supplies. Her shoulders drooped with sadness and exhaustion. She halted a few feet from him.

"My beloved, you need not come here every day." Job reached for her hand instinctively, but quickly drew it back to his side. He was afraid to touch her lest he contaminate her. He leaned upon his staff. Quietly he asked, "How was the trip?"

Tilting slightly forward, Channa placed the care basket at his swollen feet. Slowly rising, she avoided his scrutiny. She shrugged her shoulders. *"All the same, nothing changes."*

Dispassionately Channa stared at his offensive appendages. Long, bony hands and fingers protruded from his emaciated arms. As her gaze slowly traveled over him, she glimpsed a mere shadow of his former self. Loss of appetite and continual excruciating pain had resulted in extreme loss of weight. Inflamed, ulcerous sores covered his body from head to toes. There was no arrest of the persistent itching the malady generated. The sickening, open wounds assaulted Channa's senses. Skin lesions would burst open, scab over, then crack and ooze putrid, repulsive pus. All too often, worms formed in the open sores. The potshards not only eased the intense itching of Job's flesh, but also removed the offensive discharge. His skin was frail and nearly translucent. The slightest movement revealed his skeletal bones protruding through the thin cotton clothes hanging loosely from his frame. "*If he sneezes, he will fall over and break into a million pieces,*" she thought to herself, near hysteria. She unconsciously cleared her throat to regain control. Where had her strong hero gone? Who was this shell of a man before her? The ravages of the debilitating abscesses distorted his once handsome face. His eyelids were darkened and drooping. Difficulty of breathing made his voice raspy and his breath most foul.

Today was a good day for Job. His body was not plagued by the all too frequent high fever, chills and diarrhea—at least, not at this moment.

Channa shifted her gaze to the distant horizon. "I have fresh fruits, jujube tea and more water for you. And soap, clean clothes and ointment. Adah prepared your favorite soup and bread. She says she misses you and for you to keep up your strength. She is also making you a blanket."

Turning her empty gaze back to him, she observed as he awkwardly seated himself in one of two discarded chairs. He reached for scraps of potsherd to scratch the persistent itching of his afflicted skin.

"Zerah has completed the irrigation inspection. He repaired a fracture in the lines from the kitchen's outer wall to the well house," Channa reported.

The vicious snarling of three mangy dogs vying for a piece of animal carcass erupted near them. Channa's head unconsciously jerked toward their direction. Within moments, they attacked each other, fiercely fighting over the scraps of food. A spark of fear caused her throat to constrict and her eyes to widen. Job noticed her reaction and threw a rock at the fighting mongrels. Howling in surprise and fear, they fled to another garbage heap.

Looking to the edges of the muckheap, she saw outlines of shadowy figures moving in and throughout the trash piles. Until Job moved here, she had never seen the city dump nor thought about it.

They knew not that a sub-culture of denizens lived on the outskirts of this horribly filthy place. Families called the perimeter *home* and daily delved through the trash of the local citizenry. Channa had seen unwanted or unusable furniture, clothes and other possessions discarded here as well as household garbage and waste. These people survived off the debris of others.

"You have lost more weight, Channa. Have you seen the healer?" He halted the incessant scratching to look at her face.

She looked down at the loose fitting clothes. There was that dreadful headache again! She instinctively began rubbing her temples. Her weary body slightly swayed.

"Channa! Look at me."

She jerked to attention and inhaled a sharp intake of breath, her eyes wide with alarm.

"You need to sit down before you fall down. Please."

"I'm fine," she replied.

"Then talk to me. I know you. Something is troubling you. Tell me what is wrong." With great determination, he willed himself to cease scratching and painfully rose to his feet.

Try as she may, she could not stymie the fear and despair invading her soul. Channa took a deep trembling breath, tears trickling down her flushed cheeks. "When God took our children and grandchildren, it shattered my heart. I felt numb, sleepwalking through the land of the living. I wondered, 'Will I ever be able to feel again? Will I ever experience laughter or joy again? How do you resurrect the fragments of a crushed heart? And, how long will it take before I can look at a child and not break forth into tears?'" She stopped, her hands unconsciously covering her heart.

In a soft but detached voice, Channa continued. "I wanted to die, Job, to be with our children. But, how could I leave you, my husband? You needed me. Oh, how I struggled to make sense of those conflicts."

A stunned look crossed Job's face. "I never knew," he whispered.

Channa reached out to touch his face. He instinctively stepped back with a sorrowful shake of his head.

Her hand dropped to her side. Her eyes looked deeply into his. "I know. You were wrapped in your own grief. I don't remember a lot about those first few days. But I know you were busy with funeral arrangements and . . ." She paused, biting her lip. Her voice dropped to barely a whisper. "The look in your eyes after you returned with all their broken bodies . . ." With closed eyes, Channa crossed her slight arms over her heaving bosom. Slowly, she rocked herself until the tight grip of sorrow lessened its hold.

Job watched her agony, powerless to protect her. His hands clenched the staff, knuckles turning white. Tears flowed freely down his swollen face. Turning around, he pulled a rickety chair toward her. "Beloved one, please sit before you fall down."

Channa gratefully accepted. Using a portion of her sleeve, she tried to clean her face of tears and dust. She waited as Job once more seated himself.

"Please continue," he said, wiping his tears.

"God allowed us the honor and privilege to love and nurture our sons and daughters. My entire life I have known that being a wife and mother was the reason for my existence. Now, I am deprived of motherhood. All I have are memories, memories that too often shred the hollow recesses of my heart. Whenever my grief is most overwhelming, I hear a still small voice say, 'I the Lord, give and I take away.' I know in my intellect that death is part of life and it is temporary. I know when I die that God will resurrect me, and you, and all our families. No matter the avenue of death, ultimately, it is Creator God who takes us away. Death is subject to the law of the universe: the power to create life grants the power to control life. I take comfort in this truth. I deeply grieve our children and grandchildren every day and I know you do, too. I accept the pain of their absence. I really do." Her eyes never faltered from his penetrating gaze. But . . ." She lowered her head.

"But what, my beloved?" He gently probed.

She took a deep breath, raised her head and looked once more into his weary eyes. "Job, they died quickly. No suffering, no pain. And I am most thankful to the Almighty for that!" Her knuckles were turning white from the pressure of her clasped hands. Her breathing became uneven and her body tense. "But I cannot understand . . . you . . . why . . . oh, my head hurts." She groaned in frustration. "It is difficult to put into words." Her fingertips pressed into her temples.

Through his excruciating pain, he recognized the torture of her soul. "What are you struggling with, heart of my heart?" He leaned toward her, yearning to hold and comfort her. His eyes fervently searched her ashen face, seeking understanding of her inner turmoil.

She blurted out, "You are and always have been a man of great integrity. Everyone knows your unwavering devotion to the Almighty. I, more than anyone else, know your faithful and obedient heart." She closed her eyes against a fresh onslaught of tears.

The dam of pent up despair broke and the words tumbled forth. "Why, Job, why? Why must you, the paragon of integrity, suffer so brutally? You judge righteously and care for the widows and orphans. You honor and worship God with all your heart, mind, soul and strength. Why must you be plagued with this despicable affliction? Why does God not heal you or put you out of your misery? Have we offended Creator God? Why is God silent? Why doesn't He respond to our prayers?"

Job wished he knew the answer to that question. Oh how he wanted an answer from God!

She edged forward in her chair, nearly tilting it over. Her voice was terse, eyes slightly narrowed. "When you were still at home, many were the nights you cried out in pain, begging God to take your life. In your delirium you told God how cruel He was to you, how unbearable the pain, your only release being unconsciousness. You were frightened by dreams and terrified of visions. You still have them, don't you?" She glared at him, the tide of anger and helplessness, unabated. "In the most difficult times of this illness, I heard you curse the day you were born, preferring miscarriage to life, loathing the very air you breathed! However, it is not *your* life Job; it is *our* life. I am your wife! You abandoned me, Job! You packed up and *left* me! You are isolated here, away from me, away from the safety of the home we built side by side. Why must I be as a widow, bearing sorrow upon sorrow, *alone*, while you scarcely survive here in this . . . this . . . filthy miserable unhealthy pit of hell?" Channa collapsed to her knees, grief robbing her of all strength. Sobs tore from her exhausted body as she drew her shawl over her head. Her arms tightly hugged her torso as she rocked herself back and forth for comfort.

Job had no answer. Slowly and painfully, he sank to the ground and prayed for divine wisdom. His indescribable love for her motivated him to leave home and come here. He wanted to protect her, and others, from possible contagion. The continual, unrelenting torment that swept his body caused frequent shrieks in pain. There was no comfort for him, whether seated, standing, or prostrate. The delirium and sleeplessness affected them both. Channa diligently attended him day and night, sleeping whenever she could. She repeatedly cleansed the acrid discharge of the inflamed boils with linen clothes and applied her healing ointments. The effect upon her physically and mentally was weakening her. Both were still mourning their children. He left home for her sake, to shield her. It never occurred to him the effect his departure would have upon her spirit. She felt forsaken, widowed, and bereft of a husband. The revelation stunned him! He dropped his head into trembling hands. "What have I done?" He mumbled. His conscience wrestled against his heart. Shoulder-to-shoulder they built their home and reared God-honoring children. Together, they buried those same loved ones and their families. She never complained or bemoaned their loss of wealth or the prestige many attached to it. The drastic change of their lifestyle, she took in stride. She staunchly supported his plans to rebuild Shiloh, their homestead and legacy. Now, Job was stricken from head to toes with oozing, odiferous boils. For every physical blow Job was enduring, so was his beloved wife. However, the physical separation was torturing her soul beyond measure. What had Creator God told Adam in the garden? 'A man shall leave his father and his mother, and be joined to his wife; *they shall become one flesh.*' Why had he not recognized this before? They were *one*, in health and in sickness! His heart sank with that painful awareness.

Slowly, Channa's sobs subsided. Removing the shawl from her head, she wiped the tears from her swollen face. She placed her delicate hands over her heart. Looking at Job, voice barely audible, she spoke.

"We believe and taught our children that the Redeemer lives, and after death we will see God and behold His glory. My heart cannot be crushed more than it is now. Death will be a sweet release for both of us, a welcome sanctuary." Lifting her eyes heavenward, she again prayed forgiveness for her next words. Then looking straight into the pain-filled eyes of her beloved Job, she spoke. "Do you still hold fast your integrity? Of course you do. And I love you for it. But beloved, there is no dignity in an ash heap! Curse God. And die."

The silence was deafening. With bowed head and tightly closed eyes, she fearfully trembled, waiting for a bolt of lightning to fry them to the spot! One minute passed, then two, then three. No ground opening up to swallow them or force of nature to destroy them. Nothing. Not even a roll of thunder from the heavens! She hesitantly opened one eye and then the other, her breath slow and anxious. Apprehensively, she looked at Job and waited for his reaction.

Job tilted his head to one side, his forehead slightly furrowed. He knew his wife's heart; she spoke from love and despondency. He was wise enough to know that provoking remarks from one in unfathomable grief belongs to the four winds. The shadow of a half-smile creased his tired face. "Curse God? And die? You speak as one of the foolish women." Absently, he scratched an unrelenting boil, his eyes never leaving her face. "Now the kind woman I know and married and cherish is wise . . . but her thinking today is clouded by deep sorrow."

Channa lowered her eyes and breathed deeply, forcing her tensed frame to relax. How she needed her husband's clarity of mind. He was her much needed anchor and she was drifting in the Sea of the Unknown.

The sound of small children playing at a nearby trash-heap drew her attention. "Is it foolish to love another more than life itself? Is it foolish to want so desperately to ease or expunge their excruciating suffering? And is it foolish, my beloved husband, to want from God a swift death and release from all pain?" Tears trickled down her cheeks and fell on her now dirty mourning dress.

"How painful are honest words." With painstaking effort, he shifted the weight of his body. Grasping his staff with swollen hands, he slowly rose from his sitting position. Guttural moans escaped his lips.

Channa brushed back the hair falling onto her face. She stood and straightened her dress.

"Were you expecting swift judgment?" He leaned heavily on the staff for support.

She nodded her head as her hands repeatedly twisted the fringes of her shawl.

Job sought for the right words to comfort her. "My love," he paused until Channa looked into his bloodshot eyes, "shall *we* accept good from God and not accept adversity? I am learning, be it grudgingly, that suffering helps clarify my priorities. God is just. And good. He knows our hearts better than we do. He sees our intense grief. I believe that He, in His own way, shares that grief. Some things require not reasoning, but blind faith. We must endure with dignity these trials encompassing us."

A slight breeze ruffled Channa's hair. "Sit, my husband." She pulled the wooden chair to him and held it as Job seated himself. Reaching inside the nearby food basket, she withdrew tea for both of them. She placed the teacups on her chair.

Job cleared his throat. "Why do you come here, day after day, and subject yourself to the utter filth of this despicable place?"

His question surprised her. "Because you are my husband," she whispered, "it is my duty and honor."

He bent forward and grabbed his chest as a coughing spasm nearly asphyxiated him. Involuntarily, she recoiled from him. Minutes passed before he had a measure of composure. His contorted face soon relaxed and the irregular breathing eased. He leaned back against the chair, weakened by the attack. The sight of him, helpless victim to the whims of this devastating affliction, wrenched her heart. She closed her puffy eyes and with balled fists, covered them as more tears threatened to fall. The sultry, putrid air around her was nauseating her stomach. The headache was growing in intensity. She struggled for control of her raw emotions and weakened body. Willing herself to do so, she opened her eyes.

With slightly bowed head, Job edged a crusted stone toward her, using his staff to limit any physical contact.

Her gaze fell to the deformed mineral clod. Haphazardly shaped by weather and location, the stone was not distinctive. She picked it up and turned it in her hand before depositing it in her pocket.

"My dove, you must not come back here." He raised his shaking hand to halt her objection.

"Your duty to me is to heal yourself. Your duty to me is to forgive yourself for surviving. Your duty is to make *our* house a home again." His faint strength was quickly waning. "Channa, we are blessed to have been so favored by the Almighty with the stewardship of children and possessions. We have the gift of cherished memories. And we have each other."

Channa knew he was right. She missed their children—no, God's children! She missed the presence of her husband and his strength and leadership. She missed her life the way it 'used' to be. She missed the laughter and the joy in her heart and in her home. But most of all, she missed the peace that passes all understanding. Peace. Sweet peace that replaces all fear and uncertainty.

"Channa, look at me."

She gazed into his sunken and bloodshot eyes. His raspy voice continued.

"Go home. Do not return here. Elihu will bring the meals and necessary provisions to me until I return home. Do you hear me? I am coming home. Soon. Promise me that you will eat and rest properly." He tilted his head and gave her his "I-am-ever-so-serious" look.

For the first time in weeks, a slight smile crossed her lips. How she missed him. Frowning reluctantly, she nodded her head in agreement.

"My precious dove, you are in the hands of the Almighty. Rest. Recover. And learn to rejoice again." He smiled, as best he could, at her and bowed. "Shalom, my forever love."

Without a backward glance, she walked to her buggy. The faintest glimmer of hope touched her battered soul and rose to her eyes. Drawing her shawl close around her, she felt a great weight lift from her weary shoulders.

"Zerah, please see to the horse." Passing the reins to her foreman, she stepped down from the buggy. "Deliver this message immediately to Elihu. 'I have instructions from master Job.'"

Her eyes surveyed the expanse of rural scenery before her. *"Strange,"* she thought, *"how savagely beautiful is this land."* The snowcapped mountains in the far distance were indeed breathtakingly gorgeous to behold. But death awaited the unsuspecting traveler or straying animal when exposed to the freezing temperatures. Yet the melted snows provided the invaluable water so necessary to feed the rivers and many tributaries and watering holes. Beauty and danger. Life and death.

She felt Adah beside her. Glancing at her faithful friend, she smiled wistfully. When she spoke, her voice was surprisingly peaceful as was her countenance.

"I have business to take care of for now. Prepare me a light meal and then . . ." her voice trailed off. She quickly embraced her precious friend.

Taking a deep breath, she resolutely headed for the family cemetery beyond her home.

Channa fell to her knees and bowed her head in worship. *"God, forgive me. I am ashamed. I, the created, demanded an explanation from the Creator."* Tears of remorse slipped down her face as she knelt in solitude. A gentle breeze caressed her brow.

Taking the dirt-encrusted nugget from her pocket, she deliberated its condition. Why had Job given it to her? There was a reason he wanted her to have this, of that she was sure! Diligently, she began to clean its surface. Using her fingernails, she carefully removed layers of grime. The process was tedious. She spat upon it several times to aid in the procedure. With satisfaction, she held the now clean crystal up to the brilliant light. The sun's rays reflected off the deep red gemstone. It was a raw ruby! With her untrained eye, she had not recognized the worth of the camouflaged precious jewel! However, Job did!

With a small laugh, she addressed the treasure she held. *"Hello, 'queen of precious stones.' Are you indestructible? Intense heat and pressure forged you into the beauty you are now. Of course. Indeed, you are most rare and a valuable discovery. Look how the sun magnifies your luster and clarity. How did you, like my Job, come to be in the garbage heaps?"*

A chill ran up Channa's spine. Truth dawned in her soul. The reason rubies were the world's most precious gemstones was because of their rarity. They were rare because of the harsh conditions necessary to forge them. Without the pressure, there was no treasure.

With a contented smile, she placed the beautiful ruby upon the altar. *"I am beginning to understand. I thought I knew You, God. But who can know the mind of God Almighty? Forgive me for doubting and being fearful after all the gracious favor You freely bestow upon Job and me. How ungrateful I am. Today, I consecrate myself anew to You, realizing that You are sovereign, holy, and all wise. You know the way I take. You know my thoughts before I do. You set the stars in space and the boundaries of the seas. You bring life from death every spring. Only You, God, can heal and restore my body and soul. I give You myself, weary and heartsick. As surely as day follows night, I know I can trust You to bring beauty from ashes. I choose to embrace whatever circumstances or refining You deem necessary in my life. Take my thoughts, words, passions, my essence, and transform me into a brilliant ruby to mirror Your grace."* Rising from her contrite kneeling position, she hugged herself tightly then blew a kiss to heaven. Taking another deep cleansing breath, she turned from the graves before her and began her descent to home and a future.

Chapter 11

. . . a woman who fears the LORD, is to be praised. Proverb 31:30

Late afternoon sunshine spilled over the hillside as Channa took the last few steps up the knoll. Pausing for breath, she leaned heavily upon her walking stick and admired the tall, spreading cedar that Job had planted at the crest of the knoll. The shade from its bounteous boughs provided a beautiful backdrop to the hallowed graves dotting the family cemetery. Job called it a symbol of life, a memorial of our families' lives here and in the resurrection to come.

She sat beside the sacred grave of her beloved Job sheltered in the shade of the magnificent cedar. Lifting her hand, she removed the broad brimmed hat from her head. With a slight shake of her head, the tresses fell freely around her shoulders. She was weary in soul and body, but at peace.

"Any day now, my beloved, God will call me home." She sighed deeply. "I long for that moment." She surveyed their vast estate from her vantage point. Their property and livestock spread as far as the eye could see in all directions. Small dots sprinkled the landscape. These were the homesteads of four generations of family blessed by the hand of the Almighty.

"You would be proud of all our children and their descendants. Your godly heritage lives on." Looking toward the fading sunlight, she lay a timeworn hand upon his grave.

"I found your journal the other day. Some of the great-grandchildren borrowed it. Then when it was returned the maid forgot to place it with my other treasures. Hmm. How I miss Adah! She would never have made that mistake." A light breeze played with the tendrils of her gray hair. The gentle wind carried the faint but pleasing scent of pomegranate. A tender smile crossed her face.

"It seems like another lifetime when we walked through that fiery trial." Her gaze slowly encompassed the graves of their adult children and grandchildren, buried so long ago. "Our first family. We were all so young, so busy living our dreams. Are Josiah, Samara, and Cayenne still children? Will I be able to hold them and love them?" Tears rolled down her wrinkled cheeks, landing in her lap.

"Of course you can't tell me that now. Some things only God reveals, in His time. What were the words you spoke at their funeral? I had you write them down for me, remember? Just a moment . . . now I remember."

"As for me, I know that my Redeemer lives.
At the last He will take His stand on the earth.
Even after my skin is destroyed,
yet from my flesh I shall see God whom I myself shall behold,
whom my eyes will see and not another."

"That belief carried me through that torturous year." Her voice faded. She drew her shawl close around her shoulders. These many years removed from the overwhelming grief and pain of that time, she could still remember and thank God for walking with her . . . for carrying her.

"Beloved, remember my dear Keturah? She and Eliphaz received a copy of your journal after God healed and restored you. Her granddaughter, also named Keturah, married a wealthy widower from Canaan. He is said to be a godly prophet." Channa paused and took a jagged breath. "I think his name is Abraham. That sounds like a good name, doesn't it? He is a much older man with a first family. Keturah bore him six healthy sons. A copy of your journal was part of her dowry from her grandmother. I miss my dear Keturah. Recollecting that time . . . it seems as if we were part of an unfolding drama, characters on a stage. God knew you would endure the painful trials with integrity! He trusted you, beloved." Her voice was frail and fading.

"He uses your testimony to encourage generation upon generation."

Stars began to twinkle in the early night sky. She knew someone would be along soon to assist her home. She did not want to return there but desired to stay here, where she belonged, by his side.

"I'm so tired." Her breathing was shallow and labored. Her voice became a faint whisper.

"I think . . . I'll just lay . . . my head . . . on your shoulder . . . Beloved."

"Channa, many daughters have done virtuously. But you, my beloved. excel them all." Job

About the Author

Donna Dowis has been writing stories and poetry since second grade. She takes notes on whatever is available, be it paper napkins, the backs of written prescriptions or the palms of her hands. With pen in hand, she captures a mood, facial expression or way of speaking. Donna earned a Graduate of Theology degree from Temple Bible School and a Bachelor of Science degree in Psychology from Tennessee Temple University in Chattanooga, Tennessee. She also holds a Master of Christian Counseling Psychology from Christian Bible College and Seminary, Blue Springs, Missouri.

She has published poems in editions of The International Poet Society. Three times she received the Editor's Choice Awards from the Society. She has written and directed many church and community programs, and is a guest speaker or soloist at various functions. Donna is a gifted storyteller and can weave a story out of nothing or anything.

Donna is a wife, mother, grandmother and teacher-at-heart. Her passions are teaching, writing, and exploring historical locations with her beloved husband. They enjoy walking and bike riding in Chickamauga National Military Park and downtown Chattanooga, Tennessee—Donna's hometown. They are fans of the Chattanooga Lookouts Minor League Baseball team.

Between them, they have six adult children, twelve grandchildren and two great-grandchildren. They are thankful to God for every blessing bestowed upon them.

CPSIA information can be obtained
at www.ICGtesting.com
Printed in the USA
FFHW021619190519
52543053-57997FF